Famous Business Fusions

High-Impact Business Innovation Series

Edited by
CJ Meadows

Volume 1

CJ Meadows

Famous Business Fusions

Ideas that Revolutionized Industries

DE GRUYTER

ISBN 978-3-11-070293-4
e-ISBN (PDF) 978-3-11-070300-9
e-ISBN (EPUB) 978-3-11-070308-5
ISSN 2700-7847

Library of Congress Control Number: 2021941667

Bibliographic information published by the Deutsche Nationalbibliothek
The Deutsche Nationalbibliothek lists this publication in the Deutsche Nationalbibliografie;
detailed bibliographic data are available on the internet at http://dnb.dnb.de.

© 2022 Walter de Gruyter GmbH, Berlin/Boston
Cover image: etorres69 / iStock / Getty Images Plus
Typesetting: Integra Software Services Pvt. Ltd.
Printing and binding: CPI books GmbH, Leck

www.degruyter.com

Advance Praise for *Famous Business Fusions*

Figure 1: A toast to Famous Fusions!

CJ Meadows has done it again. Her insight on the world of creative leaders is stellar. If you'd like to know how world-leading companies, inventors, and innovators revolutionized their industries and fields, this book is a must-read!
— **Ted Saad**, Multi-Emmy-Award-Winning Producer, CEO and Founder, Ted Saad Media

Inspiring and empowering! I've always felt that there's nothing more noble than creating a sustainable enterprise that allows people to realize their dreams. Anyone involved in building such institutions has remarkable stories to share, and here are over 70 of them! If you want to know how famous companies, inventions, and innovators made big impact and achieved success – and maybe do the same – start your journey with this book.
— **Puneet Pushkarna**, Venture Capitalist at Solmark and Chairman of Innoveo and Servion Global Solutions

This book should be mandatory reading for entrepreneurs and innovators – whether new or experienced – employed in a company or striking out independently. Dr. Meadows has loaded the book with fascinating stories and used her extensive experience to provide practical advice. She's integrated it into an eye-opening and powerful whole. If you don't read it now, you'll wish you had.
— **Dr. Edy Greenblatt**, #1 Global Resilience Coach (awarded by Thinkers50 Global Coaches); one of the Marshall Goldsmith #100 Coaches; Founder and CEO, RestorationVacation and Execu-Care Coaching and Consulting

Innovation by its very nature runs counter to habit, convention, and rules. That's why it's called innovation and also why most of it is marginalized and forgotten. Perseverance and the confluence of events surrounding the emergence of innovation can sometimes create an opening for it to thrive and in some cases, change the habits, conventions and rules of the world. — **Dr. Karen Stephenson**, Founder and CEO of NetForm

https://doi.org/10.1515/9783110703009-202

CJ has yet again created a masterpiece with carefully chosen powerful examples to help us understand high-value innovation. This book illustrates that we understand by fission but create value with fusion. This simple idea has profound implications and points us towards the future of innovation across all industries.

– **Arun Sundar**, CXO, Venture Advisor and Board Member,
and Founder of The Social Capital Institute

The reality behind creative fusion is the theme of Dr. Meadows' new book. It's critical as enterprises everywhere try to recreate the conditions needed for creativity to take root. Insights from every field abound here – from tech to travel, from science to services. Read, Learn and Fuse! – **Dr. Chris Marshall**, AVP – Future of Intelligence, IDC

Acknowledgments

Figure 2: Thank you!

Every time I sit down to write, I pray – or, anyway, the writing is better when I do. I thank God first and foremost (see Figure 2) for every day in which I can discover, ponder, share, and either create good myself or inspire and enable others to do so. I know where my inspirations come from. The mistakes are entirely my own. Life is better with God.

My husband and children have either missed me terribly or gladly had me out of their hair while I sit in a corner and write. I have a funny feeling it might be the latter, and they'll be encouraging me to write many more books in this series. I thank Chris, Jonathan, Anna, David, and Sarah Marshall, and my brother Nishikant Mukerji, as always, for teaching me so much and for helping me grow in ways I never would have thought of on my own. I thank our helper, Gisela Cabalang, for lightening my load so I can do things like this. Life is better with family and help.

Nitish Jain and the S P Jain School of Global Management have fully supported not only the first Fusion book that spawned this series but also this book. I thank you, NJ, and the institution for your faith and excitement, research support, time, and superb marketing efforts to share these ideas with our corporate community. Business gets better with new ideas and inspiration.

I thank Eswar Krishnan and Swesha Venkateshwaran, the finest and most generous volunteer research assistants anyone could ask for. Eswar uncovered the majority of the stories shared here, thus tilling the literary soil from which this book grew. Swesha did the onerous but necessary work of reference formatting and pursued technology infrastructures for another project that freed up my time to pursue this. Work is better and more fun with a great team.

Thank you Arun Sundar, who contributed great examples and continues to evangelize Fusion Leadership Development. It's been gratifying to know that Fusion

https://doi.org/10.1515/9783110703009-203

gave you a language for what you did at TrustSphere and that you are helping other leaders grow. Evangelism is more powerful with visionary colleagues.

Thank you Stefan Giesen, Jaya Dalal, and the whole team at De Gruyter. You're always great to work with and so patient with me. Book-writing is so much better with a cohort of great professionals.

Thank you to the authors I've noted and those I've forgotten. You've shared the pieces I've assembled here in a new way. New concoctions like this book are better when others have shared great ingredients.

Do forgive me, please, if I've missed someone. Writing is better with a fantastic memory. Unfortunately, I haven't got one.

And finally, thank you, readers, for being curious enough to read this book. I hope it becomes a creative piece in a new creation of yours. The world is better, I'm sure, because of you.

Contents

About the Author

One of Asia's top ten women in information technology (IT), Dr. Meadows leads a Design Thinking and Innovation Center at a Forbes Top 20 International Business School, creating growth initiatives at the intersection of IT, business strategy, and design. Her research, consulting, and coaching focus on leadership and creativity. She co-founded an Advanced Technology Think Tank and Tinker Lab, envisioning the Future of Work (FoW) and Education, applying artificial intelligence (AI), biometrics, and other advanced technologies to leadership development, team productivity, and group innovation. She holds a doctorate in business administration and IT from Harvard Business School and has more than 20 years' experience in Asia, Europe, and North America as a consultant, coach, entrepreneur, eBusiness builder, innovation lab co-founder, and Accenture IT and Business Strategy consultant. She can be found at www.spjain.org/faculty and www.drcjmeadows.com.

https://doi.org/10.1515/9783110703009-205

Introduction and How Fusion Can Help You

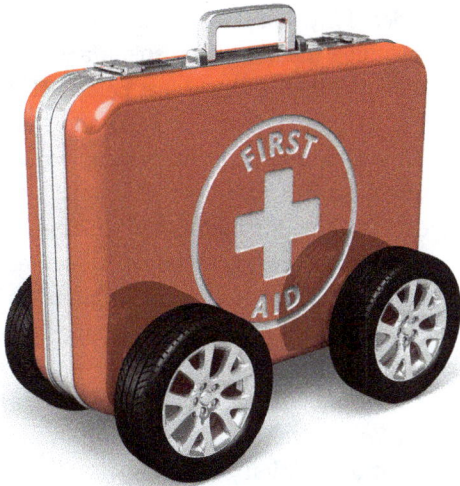

Figure 3: Can healthcare learn from a Formula 1 pit crew? Yes!

> Bringing in ideas from analogous fields turns out to be a potential source of radical innovation. When you're working on a problem and you pool insights from analogous areas, you're likely to get significantly greater novelty in the proposed solutions, for two reasons: People versed in analogous fields can draw on different pools of knowledge, and they're not mentally constrained by existing, "known" solutions to the problem in the target field. The greater the distance between the problem and the analogous field, the greater the novelty of the solutions . . . consider our recent study in which we recruited hundreds of roofers, carpenters, and inline skaters to contribute their insights to the problem of workers' reluctance to use safety gear because of discomfort. . . . Each group was significantly better at thinking of novel solutions for the other fields than for its own.
>
> – Nikolaus, Marion, and Martin (2014)

What feature did mobile phones get from toasters? Pop-ups, of course! (Hence, the cover image on this book.) Whether you can't imagine life without pop-up notifications or you *do* imagine such a life and wish for it, the concept is the same: an idea from one place, transported somewhere new, can lead to radically creative innovation.

Case in point: Hospitals and Formula 1 racing (see Figure 3). A hospital emergency-room staff hired a design thinking team to make the emergency room "better." After consideration, the combined team decided that "better" meant "faster" and "right" – giving the right treatment quickly, since a patient could die without such care. Where could they go for inspiration?

https://doi.org/10.1515/9783110703009-206

Formula 1 racing, of course! They went out for a day of racing, sat next to the pit crew, and when car-patients rolled in, they watched the crew quickly and correctly "treat" each one and send them off. They peppered one another continually with comments like, "Hey – that's a good idea! Why don't we do that? We should do that!" They gathered loads of ideas, instituted them in the hospital, and provided dramatically improved treatment, saving more lives than ever before. They didn't stop there, though. They invited the pit crew into the hospital and said, "Here's what we do. How would you do it?" Again, they gathered fresh new ideas from a previously untapped source and made life better for patients and staff.

There's actually a term for this – lateral thinking (or analogous thinking).

When this sort of thinking leads to new inventions, companies, industries, fields, and human capabilities, it's more than just thinking. It becomes lateral innovation. I introduced the concept in *Innovation through Fusion: Combining Innovative Ideas to Create High-Impact Solutions*, as well as companion audiobooks (1) *Innovation through Fusion: High-Impact Innovation Method, Stories, and Community* and (2) *Innovation through Fusion: High-Value Lateral Innovation Intro*.

So, now there's a term for lateral innovation – fusion.

The basic idea is this: nuclear fusion releases a great deal of energy when two nuclei combine. Likewise, a combination in business, science/technology, and the arts/humanities can release a great deal of value into the world.

Case in point: Martin Rothblatt introduced satellite technology into a stodgy, old industry: radio. Sirius Satellite Radio was born and evolved into Sirius XM Holdings Inc., now worth USD 25 billion.

The innovator crosses some sort of boundary – of technology, industry, nation, field, organizational silo, and so forth – and integrates ideas, people, technology, or something in a radical, new way. This type of innovation is often high value and catalyzes radical change.

People who do this are called "fusioneers." They begin their fusion journey by learning across multiple fields and building a broad array of knowledge and skills, making them also "polymaths." In fact, the founders of the world's five largest companies are (or were) polymaths: Jeff Bezos, Warren Buffett, Bill Gates, Steve Jobs, and Larry Page (Simmons, 2018). Modern examples include Elon Musk and Mark Zuckerberg. Historical examples include Marie Curie, Isaac Newton, Theodore Roosevelt, Thomas Jefferson, Benjamin Franklin, John Adams, Leonardo da Vinci, Michelangelo, Galileo Galilei, Aristotle, Marcus Aurelius, and Archimedes.

Not only do we see individual examples, but industries, too, are either merging or simply borrowing ideas from one another, such as the following (Vullings and Heleven, 2015):
– Sushi bars use the same carousel system that airports use for baggage.
– McDonald's drive-through uses similar techniques to Formula 1 pit crews.

- Inspired by mobile phone pay-as-you-go services, Norwich Union introduced *Pay As You Drive*™ car insurance.
- Boatbound uses Airbnb's business model for boat rental.
- Inspired by retractable landing gear, retired aeronautical engineer Owen Maclaren developed the first lightweight baby stroller for his daughter, who had trouble getting in and out of airplanes with existing prams.
- Vacuum design and manufacturing company Dyson adapted a design from a nearby sawmill into its products – using a high cone to spin out dust via centrifugal force.
- Wine makers have begun to protect bottles during shipping with an adaptation from the egg carton.
- Phonebloks makes their telephone components from *LEGO*®-style pieces that can be swapped out for repair or upgrade.
- Solar panels and new fixtures have been installed in phone boxes on Tottenham Court Road in London, making them into mobile phone chargers.

Beyond industries and industry-based ideas, fields themselves are merging. Biology and technology are highly respected fields. When combined, bio-tech became a fast-growing industry with high-value innovations. Not only do we see pairs of fields combining, but now whole clusters of them are creating new value. One of the fusioneers I wrote about works in *psychoendoneuroimmunology* (*PENI*).

The sort of value Fusioneers have created (the ones I studied) is outlined in Table 1. Although I set out to study innovators, I found that 90 percent of them are also entrepreneurs and/or intrapreneurs (employee-entrepreneurs crafting new business for their companies), so theirs were not only personal stories of innovation; theirs were also stories of new companies and even whole new fields. This type of innovation is powerful.

Once I started speaking and writing about fusion at the level of the leader/innovator, company, and industry, people started asking for more examples and sharing new ones with me. In the following pages, I share these with you, plus more that have been collected especially for this book. Some are famous examples you would have heard about (like Coca-Cola or Disneyland). Some are not so famous (like Legal Grounds). I include some products you have probably used (like VELCRO®) and those I hope you haven't needed (like Given Imaging).

Since my previous book on fusion focused more on the innovators themselves, this book focuses on ideas, inventions, and companies that have revolutionized industries (or are about to) – hence the title.

I hope these examples of fusion inspire you to create new inventions, companies, and more. They are meant to inspire, illustrate, and get your creative juices

Table 1: A few companies/organizations and their impact from *Innovation through Fusion Combining Innovative Ideas to Create High-Impact Solutions* (2020).

Company/Organization	Impact
Vaxess Technologies	Millions of lives and USD 16 billion/year to save with non-refrigerated vaccines
ipac securities	More than USD 15 billion under management
SwineTech	USD 8 billion/year in agriculture to save worldwide
XCyton Diagnostics Limited	10+ million lives and USD 1.2 billion/year to save worldwide
KFC, Hungry Jack's, and Domino's Pizza Australia	USD 1 billion+ business built
Nokia Ringtones and Life Tools	World's first digital music deal (pioneer in a USD 2 billion industry) and 125 million subscribers
Menulog	USD 850 million founding team
NetForm	One of the 100 most innovative firms in the world (*CIO* magazine ranking)
SensPD and BioHug	Age 0–4 intervention for 2 million people/year
Loreto Day School Sealdah and Kolkata Mary Ward Social Centre	450,000 lives improved
FutureMap and Hybrid Reality	Million-view TED Talk, best-selling books, and leading-edge consulting
Against All Odds	One of the 25 coolest companies in America (*Fortune* magazine ranking) and record-breaking publishing
Execu-Care Coaching and Consulting and Restoration Vacation	Thinkers 50 resilience pioneer and new technology to fight the USD 50 billion/year burnout epidemic
Lime.com	Multiple Emmy Awards and the first integration of TV, radio, Internet, video on demand (VoD), and mobile
Lapis Digital/Vertic	Emmy Award-winning interactive TV and digital marketing
NSW Institute of Sport	The Olympics' top score

flowing. Photographs and illustrations are provided to stimulate, amuse, enliven, and invite thought. They are more art than example, unless otherwise noted.

Even if you're not keen to create a new company or field, is fusion still a helpful concept? Yes. More than one person has approached me and said they recognized themselves in the concepts and never had a language for what they had done or validation that it is a good thing (see Figure 4).

Figure 4: You, too can harness fusion.

Some were entrepreneurs, but some were employees who had created a great deal of value at work or who had crafted unique careers that spanned multiple fields. An example of the former used the company's technology in a new way to pioneer new services, helping his company grow and even become a Harvard Business School case study. He became a C-suite executive who always had new and interesting work at hand. An example of the latter thrived as both a singer and a marketer, flourishing both by applying her full range of skills and networks in both.

Yesterday's key to success was to become the best in the world at one thing, no matter how small. However, new research (Simmons, 2018) shows that it's just as effective (not to mention much easier) to be in the top 25 percent in two or more things. A polymath "future proofs" his or her career by turning to one set of skills or another, depending on what's needed in the moment, and he or she can earn well by being a unique resource with the power to demand a premium. Actually, it's easier than ever, now, to become competent in a new skill or field, with the rise of the Internet, online learning, and new AI-enabled learning engines (for example, EdCast).

More than 10 studies show a strong correlation between the number of interests/competencies and a person's creative impact. According to a 1,500-CEO survey by the design and consulting firm IDEO, creativity is the most important leadership trait (Sato, 2013).

In sum, with mental diversity (collect the dots) and creativity (connect the dots), we create new things of value. We keep some of that value and are better positioned to do it again. In a world that is constantly changing and looking for the newer and better, innovation may be the only sensible journey to make. New ways to innovate – with new language and concepts, as well as examples of others who've been there – should help.

In that spirit, I invite you to use these new concepts and language, reflect on your own journey to date, and gain inspiration from the stories below.

I've posted some additional material on two websites – S P Jain School of Global Management (www.globalinnovation.spjain.org/famous-fusions) and my own website (www.drcjmeadows.com/famousfusions). Companion material will also be available on GnowbeLearn™ (https://learn.gnowbe.com/), where you'll be able to watch video summaries, answer reflective questions meant to spur you to action, and craft your own fusion journey as part of a community.

There are many more examples of fusion in the world, and I invite you to share your favorites with me so I can share them with others. They may be stories from the media (please share a link or book/article reference, if so) or your own story of fusion innovation past or present. Just email me at cj@drcjmeadows.com

I thank you in advance and wish you a wonderful innovation journey!

Chapter 1
Art and Music

Figure 1.1: Fusions can create timeless works of art and whole new artistic genres.

Paul Klee: Modern-Primitive Art

Fusion(s): children's, cubist, primitive, and surrealist art

Value: more than 9,000 works of art, each valued at up to USD 6.8 million

Swiss-born painter and graphic artist Paul Klee is noted for his personal, humorous work filled with the influence of dreams, music, and poetry. Art historians find his work difficult to classify, as his small-scale drawings, paintings, and watercolors deftly blend elements of children's art, cubism, primitive art, and surrealism (see Figure 1.1).

Klee grew up in a musical family and began his artistic career as a violinist. International travel awakened his visual sensibilities, and his early etchings and drawings combine elements of satire and surrealism, drawing on the work of Francisco de Goya and James Ensor. After marrying a pianist and settling in Munich (a center of avant-garde art), he befriended Russian painter Wassily Kandinsky and German painter August Macke, later joining an expressionist group that contributed significantly to the development of abstract art. Klee and Kandinsky both taught at the Bauhaus school of design, architecture, and applied arts.

https://doi.org/10.1515/9783110703009-001

Traveling to Tunisia with Macke and Louis Moilliet, he was overwhelmed by the intense light and wrote that color "took possession" of him. He deeply explored color theory, and his blending of styles no doubt informed his deeper exploration into the elements of form and design.

His Bauhaus lectures on color and form were published as *Writings on Form and Design Theory* (the *Paul Klee Notebooks*). These have been declared as important for modern art as Leonardo da Vinci's *A Treatise on Painting* was for Renaissance art.

Paul created more than 9,000 works of art, the most expensive of which was auctioned at nearly USD 6.8 million (Pereira, 2016).

Ravi Shankar: Indo-Euro "Fusion Music"

Fusion(s): Indian and European music, as well as classical and modern/"pop"

Value: new musical genre and global fame as "the most famous Indian musician on the planet"

Noted by author Paul Klee as an example of "the most powerful creative technique" – connecting two "unconnected" ideas – Ravi Shankar was named "the most famous Indian musician on the planet" by Ken Hunt of AllMusic. This fame grew over a lifetime of fusing different musical genres and influencing and collaborating with the world's most famous musicians.

Shankar grew up as a dancer touring India and Europe with his brother's dance troupe. Although beginning his arts career as a dancer, he became a Hindustani classical music composer, and in 1956 played Indian classical music across Europe and the Americas. He enhanced its popularity through teaching, performing, and collaboration with famous musicians like Yehudi Menuhin and George Harrison from The Beatles.

Harrison bought a sitar and recorded the famous song "Norwegian Wood (This Bird Has Flown)" in 1965, later taking lessons from Ravi, some of which were popularized on film. He, Shankar, and other musicians like The Rolling Stones, The Animals, The Byrds, and blues musician Michael Bloomfield (with the improvisation "East – West") popularized Indian instruments in Western music, creating "raga rock." Shankar composed music for sitar and orchestra, touring the world in the 1970s and 1980s.

Expanding his influence from music to politics, he was a nominated member of the upper chamber of the Parliament of India from 1986 to 1992 and continued to perform until he died. Nephew Ananda, great-niece Gingger, and other family members carry on the "fusion music" tradition, and Shankar's influence lives on in them, his recordings, and countless other musicians.

Apparently, sitar and guitar work well together.

Salvador Dali: Visualizing Einstein's Relativity and Collaborating with Walt Disney

> "Surrealism is as beautiful as the chance encounter of a sewing machine and an umbrella on a dissecting table."
> – Isidore Lucien Ducasse (Comte de Lautréamont), poet

Fusion(s): conscious and unconscious; surrealist painting and film; Catalan philosophy, classicism, nuclear physics, and pop art

Value: 1,500 paintings (and other works), the top seven valued at more than USD 70 million

---

Surrealist art's defining feature is its juxtaposition of seemingly unrelated things in unexpected ways. An artistic and literary movement founded in the 1920s, surrealism celebrated the irrational, unconscious mind – believed to have been suppressed by the Enlightenment and its focus on conscious rationality.

The most famous of the surrealist artists, of course, is Salvador Dali. Among his famous paintings is one that reveals his fusions beyond the canvas. *Living Still Life (Nature Morte Vivante)* was created during a period he dubbed "Nuclear Mysticism," for the relationship between quantum physics and the conscious mind, drawn from Catalan philosophy, classicism, nuclear physics, and pop art. The painting essentially depicts "dead nature in movement," that is, objects simultaneously in motion and at rest. He essentially reveals on-canvas an embodiment of the perpetually moving atom, drawing conceptually on Albert Einstein's theory of relativity and the connection between mass and energy.

Likewise, beyond-canvas, Dali and his friend Luis Buñuel Portolés developed an idea for the first surrealist film from things they had dreamed. They wrote the script in six days, filmed the 17-minute movie, and released it in Paris. *Un Chien Andalou (An Andalusian Dog)* was a major success (studied by film students even now) and ran for eight months.

In fact, he also created a short, animated surrealist film with Walt Disney, titled *Destino*.

Dali drew inspiration most extensively from dreams and the sleeping–waking state when descending into or emerging from sleep. He would often sit holding a spoon above a tin plate on the floor and relax. When he began to fall asleep, the spoon would fall onto the plate, waking him, and he would capture whatever surreal images had flown through his mind.

This technique is modified and replicated in the keys-above-the-floor powernap and other methods for fusing conscious and unconscious minds. It is terrifically useful for generating out-of-the-box ideas and has been used by restauranteurs, corporate executives, scientists, technologists, and more.

Dali produced 1,500 paintings, in addition to book illustrations, drawings, lithographs, sculptures, and theatre set and costume designs. His seven most expensive paintings have been valued at more than USD 70 million.

Apparently, surreal has real value.

Chapter 2
Biomimicry

Figure 2.1: Elephants offer both a helping hand and inspiration for robotic helping hands.

> "Nature has frequently already found elegant solutions to common problems; it's a matter of knowing where to look and recognizing a good idea when you see one."
> – Donald Ingber, Harvard Medical School, Boston Children's Hospital, and Harvard School of Engineering and Applied Sciences (see Figure 2.1)

Desert Greenhouses Inspired by Camel Nostrils and the Namibian Fog-Basking Beetle

---

Fusion(s): biomimicry (nature) and industrial applications (for example, agriculture); camels, beetles, and a new approach to agriculture

Value: annually up to 7.3 million liters of fresh water and 130,000 kg of vegetables

---

The United Nations (UN) predicts a world population of 10 billion by 2050. At the same time, climatic shifts, deforestation, drought, topsoil erosion, and agriculture

https://doi.org/10.1515/9783110703009-002

itself have led to increased desertification across the globe. A desert is defined as any place with a moisture deficit over the course of a year, today covering a third of the world's land – and growing.

With increased demand for food, water, and energy, combined with declining resources, we need a radical new approach.

Sahara Forest Project's leaders believe solving the world's envisioned food, water, and energy shortages requires an integrated approach, and they set out to develop one in the world's most inhospitable environment – the Sahara.

Where could they look for inspiration? Camel nostrils and beetles, of course. During cool evenings, camel nostril surfaces cool exhaled air and extract water vapor from that air. Similarly using temperature differences to its advantage, the Namibian fog-basking beetle climbs to the top of a sand dune at night, radiating heat from its black shell, slightly cooling the beetle in comparison to its surroundings. From inland-blowing sea winds, tiny drops of water vapor ("morning fog") form on its shell, which is then gathered in hydrophobic troughs (bumps) on its body. Before sunrise, the beetle tips its body up and drinks the water.

Sahara Forest Project's designers, wishing to create saltwater-cooled greenhouses in the Jordan desert, drew inspiration from both of these animals, using the same principle of condensation. Harnessing sunshine and saltwater, the greenhouses use to their advantage the temperature difference between surface and sub-surface saltwater. In addition, waste from each technology is used for the others in a technologically symbiotic relationship – a biomimetic ecosystem.

The approach works. The 3-hectare site is capable of producing up to 130,000 kg of vegetables per year (rivaling current industrial farming), 20,000 liters of fresh water per day, and 39 KW of solar power (to be resold to the Jordanian grid). They sell fresh vegetables to local consumers in Aqaba, feed travelers traversing the Jordan, and operate as a test-site for new ways of feeding the world despite desertification.

With biomimicry, maybe we can transform desert into dessert.

Festo: Elephant-Trunk-Inspired Robotic Arms and Hands

Fusion(s): elephant trunks and robotic limbs; human–machine collaboration

Value: 1.8 kg robotic limb that can lift up to 500 kg

Whether you're assembling parts in a factory, performing surgery in a hospital, caring for the elderly, or fixing cars in a garage (or any other type of work, for that matter), a helping hand – or robotic arm – would always be useful. Developed by an interdisciplinary team and produced by inter-organizational collaboration, Festo's award-winning robotic arm was inspired by the elephant trunk – a limb that can uproot a 200 kg tree and then delicately pluck a blade of grass. The trunk (like Festo's limb) is controlled, efficient, flexible, and precise.

Festo's limb is made of plastic and works via compressed air. Produced via three-dimensional (3D)-laser sintering, the 1.8 kg device can lift up to 500 kg. Conventional, metallic, industrial robots can move only 10 percent of their own weight. Festo's biomechatronic device learns how to move by trial and error (like a baby) and, given its adaptive, lightweight, pneumatic design, makes human–machine collaboration both easier and safer.

Based on the same technologies, the BionicSoftHand offers a more human interface. With the aid of "massively parallel learning," mistakes are made only once, and acquired knowledge is shared among all devices, essentially connecting all hands to one another.

What could you do with a helping hand (or trunk) always at hand?

Speedo Sharkskin for Olympic Swimwear and Submarines

Figure 2.2: Sharks inspire us to swim faster in more ways than one . . .

Fusion(s): sharkskin and swimwear, submarines, and aircraft

Value: 98 percent of the 2008 Olympic swimming medals and a commercially successful product

For years, submarine, swimwear, aeronautics, and other engineers have searched for ways to reduce "drag" by making objects smoother. For an Olympic swimmer, a fraction of a second increase in speed can mean winning the gold. For aircraft, boats, and especially submarines, it can mean massive energy (and cost) savings, as well as reduction in marine barnacles and detritus collecting along the hull, further reducing energy efficiency, and requiring cleaning.

So, if being smoother makes you faster, why is one of the fastest animals in the ocean rough?

Sharkskin has long been used by island natives for sandpaper, files, and more. When submarine researchers stopped to think about it, they began to test rough surfaces and found they, indeed, work better than smooth surfaces, for both drag and detritus reduction (see Figure 2.2). Basically, instead of a smoothg surface moving through water, the rough surface "holds" water in its troughs, so essentially water is moving through water.

Speedo used the idea to produce their Fastskin line. In 2008, 98 percent of the Olympic swimming medals were won by swimmers wearing these sharkskin-inspired swimsuits, later banned as an "unfair advantage." They are commercially available, however, so if you want to swim with the sharks, try a Speedo Fastskin.

The purchase may empty your pockets, but that may help reduce your drag, too.

Shinkansen: Japan's Kingfisher-Beak-Inspired "Bullet Train"

Fusion(s): the kingfisher bird and trains

Value: 30 percent less air resistance; more speed; and something valuable beyond measure: quiet

Japan's Shinkansen (bullet train) is not only the world's fastest train, but also boasts the best safety record. However, it did have one noticeable flaw. It made a loud "boom" when traveling through tunnels – disturbing to passengers, residents, and wildlife. This was caused by air trapped in front of the train, which also slowed the vehicle and made it less efficient.

The engineering team took inspiration from the kingfisher bird, which has a long, gradually broadening beak perfect for diving into water to catch fish. The beak splits the water, instead of pushing the water ahead. When the team studied the beak, redesigned the train nose, and tested their innovation, they found the train was quieter, faster, and more powerful with 30 percent less air resistance.

Apparently, flying into water and into our imagination can help us fly on land.

Slug-Slime-Inspired Surgical Superglue

Fusion(s): the Dusky Arion slug and medical adhesives

Value: radical innovation in a USD 9.3 billion market

Andrew Smith, Professor of Biology at Ithaca College in New York, found a Dusky Arion slug in his backyard. When he picked it up, he found his fingers glued together. Although this particular species maintains a mucus coating to stay moist, when threatened by a predator, it adds certain proteins to the mucus, making a glue that prevents itself from being carried off.

Neat trick, huh? Wouldn't it be great if Band-Aids® could stick as well on wet skin? Since Smith had spent years studying biomimicry-glues, he realized this could be a perfect medical adhesive.

Thanks to further research at the Wyss Institute for Biologically Inspired Engineering and Harvard University's John A. Paulson School of Engineering and Applied Sciences, now you can do just that and more. Their new slug-inspired medical glue has two layers – a sticky surface and a stretchy hydrogel matrix. Together, they are biocompatible and bind to tissues with more than three times the strength of other medical adhesives – comparable to the body's own cartilage. Further, when used on living, moving tissues, the sticky-and-stretchy material causes no damage to surrounding tissues (unlike super glue and commercial thrombin-based glue).

This is a radical innovation in the global medical adhesives market, estimated to be a USD 9.3 billion market in 2018 (Grand View Research, 2019).

Beyond Band-Aids®, the material could be used as an internal surgical adhesive patch, injectable solution, adhesive for medical devices or soft robotics, or – if made from self-absorbable biodegradable materials – a new vehicle for drug delivery.

If these researchers stick to their work, the possibilities could be endless.

Whalepower: Whale-Inspired Turbines

Fusion(s): humpback-whale tubercules and wind-turbines, fans, and more

Value: wind turbines that use 25 percent less energy to produce 20 percent more power

---

Sharks are not the only animal to inspire us with a new approach to "drag." The humpback whale has long enthralled whale watchers with its breeching and acrobatics, despite its cumbersome 30-ton size.

How? The front edge of their fins hosts 10 or more tubercle bumps, which simultaneously increases lift, reduces drag, and prevents "stall" (loss of forward momentum). This makes the humpback the most maneuverable of the large whales and helps them catch bigger, faster prey and swim in tight circles to herd krill when they hunt in groups, feeding with "bubble nets."

Biologist Frank Fish (yes, that's his real name) placed a four-meter-long fin (from a dead beached whale) into a wind tunnel and saw for himself that the limb was exceptionally aerodynamic. Fish is now President of WhalePower Corporation, which developed and patented Tubercle Technology (TT). The company's leaders come from various fields, including biology, computational fluid dynamics, and complex fabrication.

Wind turbines using the technology are commercially available and use 25 percent less energy to produce 20 percent more power. The blades are quieter than conventional blades and may be the most efficient ever made. TT has been used on small turbines, as well as fans for large-scale high-volume low-speed (HVLS) fans, cooling towers, diesel engines, and even computer graphic cards. WhalePower licenses the technology to other developers and manufacturers, and future applications may include compressors, low-flow hydro generation, marine thrusters, mixers, and pumps.

Who would have imagined that sustainable energy for our planet could stand on the shoulders of humpback whales?

Chapter 3
Consumer Products and Retailing

Figure 3.1: Gorilla glass not only improved windshields, but also enabled iPhone "magic".

Apple and Corning: Gorilla Glass for Car Windshields and Mobile Phones

Fusion(s): Car windshield glass and mobile phones

Value: pioneering a USD 8.2 billion industry and enabling iPhone "magic"

What on earth do car windshields have to do with the iPhone?

About six months before the iPhone's launch, Steve Jobs had been using an early prototype and realized the plastic display might get scratched by users' keys and coins. So, he called Corning's CEO and asked for a new scratch- and breakage-resistant glass cover.

Although Corning usually needs two years of research and development to develop a new product, Corning had worked in the 1960s on stronger glass for car windshields – a technology never released into the market (see Figure 3.1). They later rolled that technology into new glass for laptops and TVs. It became the backbone for the new iPhone glass, dubbed Gorilla Glass.

https://doi.org/10.1515/9783110703009-003

Gorilla Glass defined the user experience of fingers on a glass touchscreen. Software response was rapid and smooth, and it became part of the iPhone's "magic." Other smartphone manufacturers followed, and in the following decade, Corning delivered 58 square-miles of Gorilla Glass – about 28,000 football fields.

Later iPhones incorporated Gorilla Glass onto the back of the phone, enabling wireless charging. Apple invested USD 200 million in Corning to help it further develop such glass – part of its partnership with other companies to help them innovate, making this a story of not only windshields and iPhones but companies helping one another, as well.

With Apple's help, Gorilla Glass pioneered the scratch-resistant glass market, predicted to reach nearly USD 8.2 billion by 2025 (Grand View Research, 2017).

By working together, Apple and Corning saw through windshields, toward the iPhone, and into the future.

Amazon: The Internet Bookstore (and More)

Fusion(s): Internet and bookstore (later, marketplace and technology services)

Value: Amazon 1.68 trillion, Jeff Bezos' personal net worth USD 185 billion

---

On a cross-country drive from New York to Seattle, a young man hatched an idea and a business plan to combine the Internet and a bookstore. He founded the company in his garage.

It was always the plan to fold in other businesses, and, over the years, he did. Following books, he added video and audio streaming and consumer goods; transformed it into a platform for third-party sellers; and added web services, cloud computing, and artificial intelligence. The company grew organically and also acquired other companies it then integrated into the parent firm.

Now, it is the world's largest online sales business, Internet company (by revenue), cloud-services provider, and virtual-assistants provider.

Combining these elements made him the richest man in the world (now surpassed by Elon Musk) and the first centi-billionaire.

Named for a mighty river with 1,100 tributaries, Amazon has tributaries, too. More than 575,000 employees, a variety of technologies, and countless partners join together to create USD 386 billion of value (revenues) per year.

Who knows who will join or where they will flow next?

Coca-Cola: Tasty Medicine

Figure 3.2: From coca leaves and cola nuts to a USD 232 billion company.

Fusion(s): coca-plant and cola-nut extract; medicine and consumer beverage; corporate and partner network; for-profit advertising and free-offer (try-it-free coupons); rum and coke (the "¡Cuba libre!"); outdoor spaces and advertising

Value: USD 232 billion company

The Coca-Cola we know today began as a coke-and-alcohol tonic (see Figure 3.2). It transitioned into a coca-plant and cola-nut medicine, evolved into a consumer beverage, and then spurred a variety of innovations during its 130-year history. Sold in all but two of the world's countries, it is the third most valuable brand in the world (after Apple and Google, according to Interbrand). Its assets total USD 90 billion – more than Pepsi and Nike put together.

The brand was created by Colonel John Pemberton, who in 1865 incurred a slashing sabre wound to the chest in the last battle of the US Civil War. Instead of dying from his near-mortal wound, Pemberton healed but grew addicted to the morphine administered by his doctors. A decade after founding a pharmacy to ensure himself a steady drug supply, he searched for a cure to rid him of the addiction. He discovered coca wine, a mixture of cocaine and wine popular in France.

He developed a concentrated syrup, named it Pemberton's French Wine Coca Nerve Tonic, and advertised it as a cure-all (or cure-many, anyways), distributing it through pharmacies, where it was sold by trained professionals who mixed it with soda water (an extension to the then-current practice with fruit syrups).

Unfortunately for Pemberton, prohibition swept across his beach-head market and halted the sale of his alcoholic beverage. There was no prohibition against cocaine, however, so he reformulated his beverage and continued selling it, albeit with only about a tenth of a recreational dose of cocaine. The "intellectual beverage and temperance drink" combined ingredients from the coca plant and cola (or kola) nut and was marketed as an "invigorating" beverage, brain tonic, and cure for all nervous afflictions.

Surprisingly, Pemberton's greatest innovation may not have been the product. It may have been the distribution network – a fusion of company and external partners – perhaps the single biggest factor in the company's early and continued success. Pemberton made the syrup (still a top-secret formula), then shipped it through an extensive network of contractors and affiliates, who could freely experiment with mixtures, marketing, and delivery to suit the local circumstance. Pemberton finally died of morphine addiction in 1888, and one of his partners, Asa Candler, bought shares and rights, took over, and grew the company.

Candler immediately issued the world's first coupon – a marketing innovation we now take for granted. He distributed slips of paper that entitled the bearer to a free glass of Coca-Cola, with the idea that once people tried the product, they would become repeat customers. It worked. The customer base grew.

He also introduced the now-famous Coca-Cola logo, written in Spencerian script, later used by Ford Motor Company and Budweiser. The iconic bottle designs followed (a break from pharmacy-only selling), and after the 1898 federal tax on medicines, Coca-Cola stopped marketing itself as a medicine, leaving pharmacies behind for good. It became merely a refreshing beverage and was marketed with emotional messaging (much later culminating in the "A Coke and a Smile" campaign).

Although the source of significant innovations listed (and not listed) here, the company cannot claim to have invented Santa Claus. The roots of the figure lie in Saint Nicholas ("Saint Nick" or "Sinterklaas"), an early Christian bishop of Greek descent and patron saint of children, noted for gift-giving. However, Coca-Cola did popularize him as a jolly fat man in a red suit (his most predominant imagery today), in order to promote drinking a cold beverage (you know which one) during winter.

In pursuit of brand-building, the company began plastering unused outdoor surfaces with advertising, thus popularizing outdoor advertising.

In 2012, with the export agreement to Burma, Cuba and North Korea were the only remaining countries where the drink was not legally sold. However, as luck (and black markets) would have it, the first rum and Coke seems to have been mixed and served in a Havana bar in 1900, by a Signal Corps officer who toasted Cuba's recent liberation from Spain. The drink was later named for the toast – "¡Cuba libre!" – and was enjoyed by millions of people over the next century. Thus, alcohol was re-integrated into Coca-Cola.

Ernest Woodruff bought the company, took it public in 1919, and ran it for the next 60 years. Realizing that fountains were not the future of the drink, he sponsored the development of metal-topped coolers; invented the six-pack with handle; pioneered the glass-fronted vending machine; and spear-headed the campaign to spread Coca-Cola throughout the entire world, via global distribution in war time and reconstruction, Olympic sponsorship, and even into space aboard the Space Shuttle *Challenger* on the anniversary of the billionth bottle.

By some measures, Coca-Cola is the most widely distributed product in history, with 1.9 billion servings consumed each day.

Not bad for a coca-plant and cola-nut drink.

Lego: Play System

Fusion(s): system and play; toys and other industries (amusement parks, resorts, film and TV, and so on); adult business and child-like play; words into a new brand name

Value: USD 6.9 billion brand name covering 600 billion toy-pieces

Systems are predictable and boring, right? Nothing you'd want to play with – unless you create a play system.

Ole Kirk Kristiansen, a carpenter from Billund, Denmark, began making wooden toys in his workshop in 1932. Two years later, he named his company Lego, a fusion of the Danish words "leg godt," meaning "play well."

In 1946, he ordered a plastic-injection-molding machine at an exhibition and began making plastic toys. Three years later, he enhanced the design of the Kiddicraft Self-Locking Bricks that had been given out at the exhibition (inspired by traditional stackable wooden blocks) and began making "Automatic Binding Bricks." On a business trip to England in 1954, Ole's son Godtfred had a chance conversation with a department-store head who bemoaned the lack of any system in toys.

So, Godtfred decided to combine system and play. That year, Lego started producing a play system that would develop children's imagination and creativity through town planning, traffic safety play, and constructing buildings.

Kids wanted to make skyscrapers, but they fell apart when moved. With the introduction of tubes inside the bricks in 1958 (after five years of materials research and development), the bricks became interlocking. With high-quality manufacturing, children could interlock the bricks into new creations, take them apart, and make something else again and again. Combining plastic and building blocks in an easy-to-use way was a hit.

By 2015, Lego had produced 600 billion Lego parts and replaced Ferrari as the "world's most powerful brand." Investing in collectible Lego sets yielded greater returns than investing in gold, and Lego became the biggest tire manufacturer in the world (by number of tires).

In 2019, the Lego brand was valued at USD 6.9 billion. The company now includes amusement parks and resorts, board games, books and magazines, clothing, films, manufacturing, retail stores, TV, and video games. Innovation continues with initiatives like business consultancy, via "Lego Serious Play," which fosters adult creative thinking through a melding of business and play.

What *will* they play with next?

L'Oréal: The Science of Beauty

Fusion(s): science and beauty; beauty categories; spokespeople multicultural, multiracial, multi-gender, and multigenerational; virtual and physical; global internal, external, and joint-venture operations

Value: USD 183 billion 100-year-old company spanning 130 nations, offering more than 80,000 products across 25 brands

L'Oréal was founded to combine the very separate worlds of science and beauty and to continuously create innovative new consumer products.

They've done well. L'Oréal has famously mastered a broad variety of beauty categories from luxury to mass-market – cosmetics, cosmeceuticals, hair care, fragrance, skin care, and more, leveraging strengths in each to serve the others. Their range of spokespeople is multi-cultural, multi-racial, multi-gender, and multi-generational.

Their digital approach is similarly diverse and integrative. Consumers can watch YouTube videos demonstrating product application, avail themselves of useful expert advice, use try-before-you-buy interactive apps on mobile and laptop, and partake of sampling programs and vending-machine kiosks. In fact, via the "foundation matchmaker" at lorealparisusa.com, the company can recommend a drugstore shade of L'Oréal foundation to replace your current department-store brand and shade, integrating different brands and sales channels from the customer's perspective. Who else matches this level of inter-brand, inter-channel, brick-and-click integration?

Organizational integration is key, as well. L'Oréal creates more than 7,000 new products each year, and each innovation step is well-orchestrated, from laboratory to eco-friendly functional packaging to sales – worldwide. Packaging coordination, for example, is both internal and external, from marketing to packaging design to supplier, and must be coordinated globally. Each innovation must adhere to a global brand and product concept but face (no pun intended) different local suppliers, plants, stock and custom tools, strategies, and consumer preferences. The ultimate customer preference, of course, is to find exactly what he or she wants – hopefully fitting the company's preference – and that it's offered nowhere else and can be the foundation (pun again – sorry) for an ongoing customer relationship.

Not only does the company coordinate tightly with suppliers and distributors, but it also created a highly successful joint venture – Galderma Laboratories, its dermatology branch – a collaboration between L'Oréal and Nestlé.

Has the fusion succeeded? Yes, indeed. After 100 years in operation, L'Oréal is worth USD 183 billion, operating in more than 130 nations, offering more than 80,000 products across 25 brands. The world's largest cosmetics and beauty company, they are the world's top brand in color cosmetics, fragrances, and skin care and are second only to Procter & Gamble in the global cosmetics market overall.

That's the beauty of science . . . and the science of beauty.

Nike: "Last Foot" Personalization

Figure 3.3: Nike puts its best foot forward – lots of them!

Fusion(s): personalization and mass-production (mass customization); device/consumable/ digital-service; producers and consumers

Value: 30 percent to 50 percent premium price over existing products, deeper customer relationships, and crowd-sourced design ideas

---

Nike has integrated virtual personalization and mass-production in a very tangible way – with the mass-customized "Nike by You" shoes (see Figure 3.3). It can include a device, a consumable, and a digital service (activity, context, history, physiology, and preferences) and be continuously adapted and enabled through user data. Just go to the Nike-by-you portion of their website in your location and start designing your own shoe! If you're in one of the served markets, it'll show up on your door in two to five weeks.

The service has been wildly successful, and customers happily pay 30 percent to 50 percent more for these custom shoes. The online service has been extended to physical retail studios and an app. Having started in the US, it is now offered to consumers in Australia, Canada, China, France, Germany, Italy, Japan, Spain, and the UK.

Not only do consumers get exactly what they want, but they learn about shoe design in the process from Nike's perspective and can access recommendations from professional designers. Nike and its customers work together to produce something consumers really want, and the company is exposed to crowd-sourced design ideas.

If you find a way to co-create with customers to make wildly successful premium products, I guess you should . . . just do it.

P&G and NineSigma: Electronic-Polymer Clothing

Fusion(s): textiles and computer-chip polymers; open innovation

Value: new-product development at P&G; NineSigma's open innovation platform, hosting 2 million organizational contacts and their ideas and technologies

---

What do wrinkly shirts have to do with computer-chip polymers?

Procter & Gamble (P&G) wanted to reduce wrinkles in freshly (electrically) dried shirts and reached out to its idea-community with a broader question. Deeper and broader questioning is step #1 in radical innovation.

P&G asked not "how to make fabrics less wrinkly from the dryer," but instead asked how to "relax surface tension of organic material." Expanding the question enabled them to cast a wide net and find a connection in a field where they otherwise wouldn't have thought to look.

They crafted a radical solution, beginning with a polymer invented by a European-university computer-chip expert. It worked!

Open-innovation company NineSigma helped them redefine their question and applied it to their global database of more than 2 million contacts in companies, not-for-profits, and university labs. Their consultants search the platform for useful technologies and ideas for their clients, across industries, technologies, fields, nations, and more. They have made more than 75,000 connections between sources and clients, across 120 technical domains.

Clients can do this themselves but often find it hard to do so, given the need for problem redefinition, broad scanning, integrative/entrepreneurial mindset, and incentives (or lack thereof). NineSigma is a strong proponent of crafting open problem statements, talking with suppliers/customers/universities, scouting technology, attending conferences, talking with experts, and naturally giving as much back to those contacts as they contribute.

They also advocate broad-scanning "SWAT" teams to collaborate with others outside one's industry. Although they don't involve "special weapons," they do involve special "tactics" and speed. Such teams often unearth radical approaches from totally unexpected sources.

In P&G's case, radical reaching seems to have unearthed a new wrinkle.

PepsiCo: From Osteoporosis to Low-Sodium Treats

Fusion(s): osteoporosis research and snack foods

Value: healthier snacks with a salty taste but 25 percent to 40 percent less sodium

---

A few years ago, PepsiCo's executives posed a challenge to the research and development department: reduce the sodium in snack foods while maintaining the salty taste consumers want. After working in their own labs and searching across the packaged-food industry for ideas, they finally found what they were looking for, but in an unexpected place – a global osteoporosis research lab.

The osteoporosis researchers were particalizing and re-growing calcium, which gave PepsiCo's food scientists a new idea. Once they developed a new method for producing low-sodium salt-like nanoparticles, they were able to reduce snack-food sodium by 25 percent to 40 percent while maintaining the salty taste-profile.

It seems PepsiCo's researchers are really worth their salt.

Ralph Lauren: Mass Class

Figure 3.4: Haute couture quality meets mass (or almost mass) affordability.

> "Polo's design excellence works in concert with its disciplined business approach, and these two traits together have allowed the Company to set the standard for the industry."
> – Reference for Business

Fusion(s): creative design and business; haute couture quality and mass market sales; men's shirts and women's cut; co-leadership; internal–external operations; sales/media channels; eco-materials corporate-start-up innovation

Value: USD 5 billion company with revenues of USD 6 billion annually

Clothing salesman Ralph Lifshitz (who later changed his surname to Lauren) tired of selling "other people's neckties." With no experience in fashion design (but plenty in New York's fashion industry), he signed a manufacturing contract with clothier Beau Brummell for a new line of neckties, which he branded Polo.

He sold his ties out of a single drawer in the Empire State Building, delivered his goods to boutiques himself, and soon signed an exclusive contract with Bloomingdale's. He was the first designer with his own in-store Bloomingdale's shop.

Lauren knew nothing of fabrics, measurements, or tie-making but was a good salesman with a passion for quality. Once he founded a company with his brother and expanded to shirts, suits, and sportswear, he combined the high quality of haute couture with mass-market pricing and classic designs that would last beyond a mere season. His stylish-classic designs were lauded by fashion critics, and mass class was born (see Figure 3.4).

In a highly unorthodox move, he launched a line of men's shirts cut for women, and quickly sold millions.

Unfortunately, rapid popularity and business growth did not translate into profitability, and the company almost folded (pardon the pun). Lauren brought in a partner and divided the work between the more creative aspects Lauren loved (design, advertising, and public relations) and the business management and leadership (basically, everything else). Co-leadership worked.

Internal–external arrangements also worked well. The company licensed manufacturing, distribution, and sales to partner companies, which in turn agreed to fund part of the advertising and brand-building efforts. In some cases, partners led sales expansion, as Cosmair did with Polo fragrances.

The company expanded into shoes, accessories, eyewear, fragrances, childrenswear, luggage, housewares, and more, building a "complete lifestyle" brand. Lauren was the first to simultaneously launch men's and women's fragrances, and the housewares line of more than 2,500 products was the largest ever created by a fashion designer. Lauren also pioneered multi-page magazine advertising, setting a dreamy-nostalgic mood, showing wildly attractive, wealthy people relaxing in their Polo-wear amidst their country-estate polo housewares or on African safari.

Tight coordination with partners wasn't always successful, however, and some distributors resisted the company's insistence that an entire line of products be retailed to "maintain its integrity as an integrated whole." Lauren did rectify partner problems, but eventually launched their own retail stores and outlets in order to expand with sufficient control. International expansion and restaurants followed, as did a multi-media joint venture with NBC (RL Media) for advertising and online shopping.

Most recently, the company acquired a minority stake in an environmental-materials technology start-up that aims to revolutionize natural-fiber processing (for example, cotton waste) for high-performance materials.

Critics scoff at the company's range of product lines, brands, channels, and pricing, and to be fair, these can cause partner resentment and consumer confusion if not managed carefully. Some insist that trendy designs changing with each season or year is necessary in the fashion industry, and younger consumers prefer stylish over classic. However, Lauren built the brand on stylish-classic design and would risk losing its existing clientele if it abandons "classic" in order to compete in a crowded industry filled with "styles" that will never become classic.

The integration of stylish and classic, as well as quality and affordability, are foundational to its success.

How successful has it been? The company today is worth more than USD 5 billion, and revenues top USD 6 billion annually. The 2019 fiscal results show an increase in revenues, and leveraging its 25,000-person workforce, it operates approximately 500 stores and 600 concession shops, with partners operating nearly 300 more for millions of consumers worldwide.

Being in a class of your own needn't mean you're alone.

Ramraj: Velcro Dhotis

Fusion(s): traditional-wear (dhoti) and modern convenience (VELCRO®)

Value: modern-traditional clothing available in more than 2,500 outlets; keeping culture alive? priceless

---

Mahatma Gandhi (1869–1948) famously wore a traditional half-dhoti, folded as the farmers do, between the legs (to avoid mud). Seventh-century kings wore them, and in modern times, poets, writers, intellectuals, and political leaders have long been seen as dignified when wearing their full dhotis and veshtis (worn like a sarong). Made of four or eight yards of cloth in cotton, silk, or a blend of both, the style of wearing used to reveal the wearer's occupation, caste, and income. Now, the younger generation wears them mainly to weddings and festivals.

Surprisingly, some hotels and restaurants refuse entry to dhoti- and veshti-wearers. On one such occasion, when K.R. Nagarajan sat outside under a tree while his friends ate inside, he decided to change perceptions and founded Ramraj Cotton.

Advertising his brand of dhotis as a fashion statement, his models enter banks and high-rise buildings, receiving welcoming salutes. To make the already-comfortable garments convenient, he integrated a modern element – VELCRO® – and introduced a line of veshtis for children.

Daily sales exceed 5,000 and are now available in more than 2,500 clothing outlets and 55 company-owned retail stores. Nagarajan has plans in place for business expansion and conversion to a public limited company.

The Genxt pocket dhoti is especially popular with grooms, who can now "tie the knot" without worrying the dhoti will slip off a hip. He's secure, in more ways than one.

Walmart: Vendor-Managed Inventory

Fusion(s): supplier–retailer integration

Value: core competence of the world's top retailer, worth USD 412 billion

---

The world's top retailer competes with collaboration.

With Walmart's vendor-managed inventory model, suppliers directly access current inventory and logistics data and manage the inventory themselves, instead of passively standing by for orders. They see how much is in stock, track the rate of sales, and decide when to send products to Walmart's warehouses. Warehouse-to-shelf is managed by the retailer.

In fact, goods often don't make it into the warehouse, with "just-in-time cross-docking." Supplier trucks meet the retailer trucks at Walmart's warehouse and shift goods directly from truck to truck for store delivery.

Not only is the supply chain more efficient, but Walmart minimizes inventory cost and shifts the cost of inventory management and purchasing onto suppliers. Suppliers and retailers both benefit from low retail prices (due to cost savings) and being able to respond rapidly to changes in demand, ensuring that goods are where they need to be when customers want them.

Although not the only element in Walmart's success, supplier integration is the core of all the company's strategies. Initiatives across the entire business either support or exploit their cost- and responsiveness-advantage, based on inventory and logistics.

How successful has it been? Walmart is now the world's leading retailer with more than USD 500 million annual revenue and more than USD 412 billion market capitalization.

Everyday low prices from everyday integration.

Chapter 4
Entertainment

Figure 4.1: Pulling two threads together can be quite entertaining.

Chuck E. Cheese's: The Amusement Park Restaurant

Fusion(s): restaurants and arcade/amusement-park entertainment

Value: USD 1.4 billion company that spans more than 600 locations

Once you've co-founded a technology company, what would you do next? Open a restaurant, of course! But, of course, it couldn't be just an average food company. It would have to launch a whole new category.

That's just what Atari co-founder Nolan Bushnell did when he created Pizza Time Theatre, with its robotic, cigar-smoking mascot, Chuck E. Cheese (CEC) (for which the business was eventually named). In fact, the new venture was originally part of Atari. In an era when arcades brought to mind teenagers getting into trouble, Bushnell wanted to give arcade games a more family-friendly image. Parents wanted to sit and enjoy a meal. Kids love pizza and want to play.

So, a new category of restaurant-play was born.

CEC now has a market capitalization of USD 1.4 billion and 612 locations.

https://doi.org/10.1515/9783110703009-004

Does this mean we can play with our food, now?

Cirque du Soleil: The Broadway Circus

Fusion(s): circus and a variety of entertainment genre; art, technology, and business

Value: USD 1.5 billion company – the world's largest contemporary circus producer; USD 845 million to USD 1 billion annual revenues

---

Originally founded by a creative band of street performers, Cirque du Soleil began its innovation journey by asking for feedback from its circus audience. Faced with a substantially negative reaction, they challenged their perceptions of what a performance should really be and reached into other industries for inspiration: ballet, cabaret, music concerts (including opera), street performance, theatre, and more (see Figure 4.1).

From this mix of influences, they created a new category – theme-led shows – with amazing acrobatics, beautiful costuming, compelling stories, dance, lighting, music, and staging. One of their first productions was titled "We Reinvent the Circus."

They moved beyond the unprofitable children's market and began serving adults and corporate clients who could pay a premium price for an unprece-dented experience. As a company, they built a culture of innovation, starting with hiring a diversity of people, and encouraging them to search for new chal-lenges, debate, develop, and use creative dissent to quickly eliminate bad ideas and spur breakthroughs. Now, they have an extensive archive of thousands of books, images, music, and videos with which to create.

They partner with others, including university engineering and art depart-ments, constantly seeking new ideas and experiments. They've partnered with Disney to create new shows, Reebok to create a fitness routine, and Bell Media to develop content for TV, videos, digital media, and gaming – including a three-dimensional feature film. They expanded their services to include private and corporate events with specially choreographed content.

Their repertoire includes both touring and static shows – 33 of them, of which 21 are still touring, with themes ranging from aquatics to The Beatles to insects to martial arts to humanity's evolution.

Today, they are the world's largest contemporary circus producer, valued at USD 1.5 billion. They've entertained nearly 150 million people in 300 cities across six continents and earn from USD 845 million to USD 1 billion in reve-nues a year.

Street performance just got a whole lot bigger. Now, it rises like the sun.

Dilbert: Office Fun

"All who know where the blame will go raise your hands."

Figure 4.2: Office humor: either laugh or cry, but don't sit there bored!

Fusion(s): humor and business culture; past and future career

Value: one of the most popular comic strips of all time, best-selling books, and a career the author loved

---

An economist by training and an office worker in big business, Scott Adams worked first in a bank and then at Pacific Bell Telephone Company. He set his alarm to ring at 4:00 am every morning for a period of personal exploration to craft a new career for himself (see Figure 4.2).

Cartooning was the most successful of the activities he tried, despite the mixture of occasional publications and publisher refusals. An inspirational letter from a fan convinced him to continue.

In his nine years at Pacific Bell, many of his co-workers became the inspiration for his cartoon characters. Three years into his telecommunications career, he signed a contract for Dilbert with United Media.

Adams included his email address in the cartoon panels and received reader feedback that helped him improve and grow Dilbert's popularity over time. Two years later, it was published by 100 newspapers. Three years after that, the total was 400.

Once the total reached 800, he became a full-time cartoonist and soon afterwards published his first book (a best-seller), *The Dilbert Principle*. Awards followed, as well as a TV series, a food company, two books on religion, and a restaurant, in a mixture of failures and successes. He became a trained hypnotist and credits affirmations for many of his successes, envisioning a goal in his mind and writing it down 15 times a day.

Without an art degree but with patience, persistence, and a continual quest to improve the craft he loved, Adams created for himself a highly unique career. The insights he portrayed and the humor so appreciated by millions of office-worker readers leveraged his past and integrated it into a future he deeply desired.

To this day, Dilbert remains one of the most popular comic strips of all time, and laughter remains one of the most powerful things any worker can do.

Disney and Pixar: The Technology and Business of Art

Fusion(s): still art combined into sequential animation; animation and live action; animation and sound; greyscale cinema and technicolor; music and video; art, technology, and business; failure and success; large and small organizations

Value: USD 366 billion (Disney) and USD 7.4 billion (Pixar's 2006 purchase price by Disney)

Disney and Pixar approached the art – technology – business innovation sweet spot from different directions: Disney from a foundation in art, and Pixar from a foundation in technology. However, the two have met well in that sweet spot, building creatively on the initial foundations laid nearly 100 years ago.

Artist and animator Walt Disney created a short film in 1923 called *Alice's Wonderland*, featuring a live actress interacting with animated characters. All animation was initially produced from still images hand-drawn and -painted by artists, sequenced into moving images via a painstaking film-making process.

After the bankruptcy that year of his Laugh-O-Gram Studio, Walt moved to Hollywood with just USD 40 in his pocket to join his brother Roy. They still believed in animation and would try again. Together, they founded Disney Brothers Cartoon Studio.

They produced further Alice comedies, which ultimately failed, and then began a cartoon series featuring Oswald the Lucky Rabbit. Unfortunately, since Universal Pictures owned the character, Disney only earned a few hundred dollars. Not so lucky for Disney.

In 1928, while on a train, Walt created an idea for a mouse named Mortimer and illustrated him. Walt's wife, Lillian, didn't like the sound of "Mortimer Mouse," so he was renamed Mickey. The firm began to experiment with animation-sound films, producing two, and then created a breakthrough.

Released in 1928, *Steamboat Willie*, starring Mickey Mouse in his first sound production, was an immediate success, not only because of Mickey's charisma, but also because it was the first mass-marketed, synchronized-sound cartoon.

The Mickey Mouse Club was founded at the request of a theatre manager, and test comic strips were sent to publisher William Randolph Hearst, later to be published in the *New York Mirror*. The cartoon company was reorganized as Walt Disney Productions, and a merchandising division and investment holding company (for real estate) were integrated into the mix. Disney was growing and adopting new, broad-based activities.

In 1932, Technicolor became the next technological advance to fold into the animation business, and soon Walt was planning his first feature-length animation, to appeal to both adults and children.

Snow White and the Seven Dwarfs took three years to complete, premiered in 1937, and two years later became the highest-grossing film of all time. *Fantasia* was released in 1940, integrating music and video well before MTV and 1980s music videos, and again integrating live-action and animation, which would be a key feature of a later success, *Mary Poppins* (1964).

Having pioneered multi-dimensional perspective-imaging with *One Hundred and One Dalmatians* (1961), the still-art, hand-sequencing process nonetheless remained manual, labor-intensive, and time-consuming.

With advances in computer technology years later, Lucasfilm (founded by George Lucas, of *Star Wars* fame) began Lucasfilm Computer Division. In this leading-edge group, New York Institute of Technology's (NYIT's) Alexander Schure (who also owned a traditional animation studio) founded The Graphics Group in 1979.

He recruited computer scientists to create the world's first computer-animated film. Located in a two-story garage, Schure invested USD 15 million into the group and gave them everything they desired, driving NYIT into financial distress. They realized they needed to produce a real film. Cinema legend

Francis Ford Coppola invited one of the early team members to a three-day media conference, where Coppola and Lucas shared their vision of the future of digital films.

Funded by Apple co-founder Steve Jobs (its majority shareholder), the group spun off seven years later as Pixar and developed many of the rendering and other technologies that would later define and foster computer animation as a field. Disney bought and used the Pixar Image Computer and software, custom-developed as part of their Computer Animation Production System (CAPS) project.

Toy Story, produced by Pixar and released by Walt Disney Pictures in 1995, was the world's first computer-animated feature film. Since then, Pixar has produced 22 feature films, 15 of which are included in the 50 highest-grossing animated films of all time.

After a successful history of collaboration between the two companies, Disney eventually bought Pixar for USD 7.4 billion, making Steve Jobs (80 percent owner of Pixar) Disney's largest shareholder (at 7 percent, above ex-CEO Michael Eisner's 1.7 percent and Roy Disney's 1 percent). Disney agreed to ensure that both companies (and their cultures) would remain distinct but synergize effectively.

Pixar's feature films have earned approximately USD 14 billion, with an average gross of USD 680 million per film, some earning more than USD 1 billion per film.

After a successful history of leading-edge animation innovation, Disney diversified into a global, multi-media powerhouse, including animation and live-action productions, broadcasting, music, radio, merchandising, publishing, streaming, theme parks and resort hotels, cruise lines, theatre, video games, and web portals. The company owns and operates ABC broadcast network, as well as cable TV networks such as the Disney Channel, ESPN, National Geographic, and others. Mickey Mouse is one of the world's most recognizable characters.

Disney earns USD 70 billion in revenues per year, employs 223,000 workers, and enjoys a market capitalization of USD 257 billion.

Significantly, both companies (Disney and Pixar) have maintained their own cultures, while leveraging the strengths of each – large and small; old and young; artistically based and technologically based; distributor and creator (although Disney maintains its own creative engine). They have both created and adopted advances in art/animation, technology, and business models in ground-breaking ways.

Who knows what they'll bring to life next?

Disneyland: Fantasy and Reality for Kids and Adults

Figure 4.3: It's a world of whimsey, a world that's real . . .

Fusion(s): fantasy and reality; virtual and physical; and play for children and adults

Value: USD 28.7 billion annual revenues for Disney parks, experiences, and consumer products (which are very popular at the parks and well-marketed there)

Disney's virtual creations are legendary, but they weren't enough for the great animation master. He wanted to create a real, physical experience of his virtual world. Existing "amusement parks" at the time were vulgar, unsanitary, and involved a great deal of beer drinking. Walt's vision, on the other hand, was a venue where his cartoon characters could come to life and interact with visitors in a family-friendly amusement park where both adults and children could play (see Figure 4.3).

An idealized version of Main Street, USA, would be the entry point and hub to four "dream" theme areas in which people could temporarily escape the realities of daily life. With horse-drawn carriages, 1900s-style fire trucks, and steam-powered locomotives, Main Street would give young guests an experience of the past (integrating past and present) and set the tone of their journey to the dreamlands. Alcohol would not be sold in the park. The family concept, play, and fusion of cartoon and reality were unique.

That uniqueness made it difficult to gain funding, location, and support. It ultimately spurred a permanent rift between artist and dreamer Walt and his commercially oriented partner (and brother) Roy, who declared that "dreams offer too little collateral."

Walt borrowed money against his life insurance policy and bought a 160-acre orange grove in Anaheim, California near a highway, so families could travel to the park easily. On July 17, 1955, the USD 17 million project was opened to the public with 26 attractions, soon to be enhanced with 12 more.

The first two weeks were besought with difficulties. Thousands of people forged entry tickets, plumbers went on strike causing the water fountains to fail (inciting accusations of paid-drinks profiteering), security personnel were seen as unfriendly (which detracted from the dream-world experience), long lines formed in front of popular rides, and visitors paid for rides individually (which added to the waiting time). Davy Crockett was soaked by a sprinkler malfunction, Fantasyland experienced a gas leak, and the Mark Twain boat nearly capsized. Opening-week struggles were televised on national TV, and slow cash flow threatened the park's solvency.

However, Walt corrected the initial problems, and within six months the park welcomed more than 1 million visitors. He used new technology – television – to promote and raise money for Disneyland via *The Mickey Mouse Club* and *Disneyland* TV shows. Attendance climbed, and the 10-year visitor count totaled 25 percent of the US population.

Walt didn't stop with a mixture of dream and reality/animation and live action. He believed the space age should take its place in the park. Roy didn't agree, and the early meetings for such an initiative became a "skunk-works" project, with Walt and volunteer engineers meeting in the parking lot after hours. Once they designed their new vision, however, it was built, and Epcot Center became one of the park's most treasured attractions.

Disney's parks benefit from the broader activities of The Walt Disney Company, including movies, TV shows, TV channel, Broadway musicals, a cruise line, soundtracks, and a host of retail products. The park has been called the most significant amusement park in US history.

In 2019, The Walt Disney Company's revenues reached nearly USD 70 billion per year, of which the parks, experiences, and consumer products generated more than 41 percent.

Not bad for a mouse and a man who went to California with only USD 40 in his pocket – and a dream that became real.

IndianRaga: Technology and Business for the Arts

Fusion(s): art, technology, and business; classical and contemporary; novices and experts; elder and younger audiences; physical and virtual venues; and artistic collaboration across a range of genres

Value: 100 million viewers from 65 countries

IndianRaga is the world's largest platform for Indian performing arts, created to enliven and connect traditional Indian performing arts with younger generations. The platform includes education and certification in classical Indian music, crowd-sourced music and dance video hosting and promotion, and a fellowship program to develop new artists through expert mentorship – all in a fun, lively, technology-enabled way. The platform offers not only media coverage but also live venues and competitions – thus spanning both virtual and physical performance.

To date, 100 million people from 65 countries have watched IndianRaga videos (the largest social media following for the Indian arts); 3,000 artists collaborate with the platform; more than 700 videos have been released; 250 fellows are developing their skills in classical and contemporary performance across a range of genres; and the organization is located in 40 cities across 7 countries.

Rage on, raga . . .

Netflix: Mailing and Streaming Videos

Fusion(s): video rental and mail service, then videos and streaming technology

Value: USD 227 billion company earning USD 20 billion annually from 167 million subscribers

Netflix famously took over Blockbuster's business by combining video rental with mail delivery – two hitherto separate industries. Blockbuster's customers could visit any of their 9,000 stores worldwide and contribute to the company's USD 5.9 billion earnings by renting in-person and returning the rented video in-person. Or they could rent from Netflix, receive their video by postal service, and return it from the comfort of their own home (or nearby post office). Consumers preferred the post, and Blockbuster has now shrunk to one store in a small town in Oregon (no, apparently, they're not completely gone).

As remarkable as it is to take over an industry (video rentals) by combining it with another industry (postal delivery), it might be even more remarkable to do it twice. Seeing the potential of streaming technology to eliminate their newly built videos-by-mail service, Netflix created yet another fusion – with streaming technology – before someone entered the competitive scene and "Netflixed" Netflix.

Once again, the company grew, but this time not by taking over someone else's business. The new fusion grew demand with unprecedented convenience. Users now need only to log in and watch – no receiving and returning physical videos. In fact, they have more to watch, since Netflix now produces new content and drives not only its customers' viewing recommendations, but also new production projects based on its artificial-intelligence engines.

The 23-year-old company earned more than USD 20 billion in 2019 from more than 167 million subscribers and is valued at more than USD 227 billion.

What was streaming seems to have become a major river.

Chapter 5
Everyday Inventions

Figure 5.1: A cloth-trimmer inspired the lawn mower, fostering the worldwide growth of suburbs, grass-played sports, and gardened institutions.

Fax

Fusion(s): telegraph, clocks, electrochemistry, and the pendulum, followed by fusions with photocopying drums, computer servers, and cloud services

Value: USD 2.4 billion industry that facilitated the growth of physically distributed business (since faxed signatures are legally binding)

Isn't the fax just 1980s technology that drowned in the wake of email? Apparently not. According to MarketResearch.com, by 2022 the global online fax market is expected to top USD 2.4 billion.

IDC further reports that fax use is growing by approximately 25 percent, and it plays a key role in digital transformation. A well-entrenched, vital communication tool for businesses of all sizes in all industries, faxed documents are legally binding, as well as secure, since the document is not transmitted without a secure, direct connection. Further, when integrated with email and other applications, there is no longer the risk of an unauthorized user picking up a physical fax from the receiving device.

https://doi.org/10.1515/9783110703009-005

There's another reason it's not dead 1980s technology: it was invented in 1843 – just 10 years after the telegraph and 33 years before the telephone.

The original device was actually a combination of clock parts and the telegraph, put together by Scottish mechanic, psychologist, linguist, logician, clockmaker, moral philosopher, education reformer, and inventor Alexander Bain. A man of many interests, he is also known as a pioneer in applying the scientific method to the field of psychology and founding the still-revered journal *Mind,* which combines psychology and analytical philosophy.

Bain's original fax process combined electrochemistry, the telegraph, and clockwork mechanics, producing messages on chemically treated paper. He later incorporated two electromagnetically synchronized pendulums in order to send scanned images. A sending pendulum would swing over a copper picture, producing an electrical impulse each time the contact touched the copper. The receiving pendulum would produce an electrical impulse that would darken the corresponding spot on the receiving chemical-paper, producing a "scan" of the original image.

A stream of inventors later improved on Bain's fax by incorporating technologies such as the photoelectric drum and, ultimately, computer and cloud technology, bringing us to the secure image transmission we enjoy today.

Apparently, scanning a variety of fields and technologies can result in a multi-billion-dollar lasting innovation.

Lawn Mower

Fusion(s): textiles and gardening

Value: USD 28.5 billion industry that facilitated the worldwide growth of suburbs, grass-played sports, and gardened institutions

---

Rising prosperity, fueled by the Industrial Revolution, ignited a generation of middle-class gardeners. Unfortunately, the only way to cut vegetation en masse at the time was the time-consuming and cumbersome scythe, an age-old agricultural tool.

Along came Edwin Budding – educated son of a farmer, carpenter, and iron-foundry worker, with a knack for pattern-making and problem-solving. Edwin watched a textile mill machine that used a cutting cylinder to trim the irregular surface of woolen cloth.

He realized that cloth-trimming (via revolving blades and rollers) and gardens (trimmed with scythes) could be combined by mounting a trimmer in a wheeled frame, pushed by an operator, to trim grass into a "lawn" (see Figure 5.1)

These "lawn mowers" would be produced in collaboration with the owner of an iron works company, later to be franchised when they found they could not possibly keep up with demand. The London Zoo and Oxford Colleges were among the first customers, but private citizens quickly caught on to the convenience and "good exercise" offered by the new lawn mower.

Edwin's invention not only changed the face of 19th-century gardening but also had a worldwide impact on the development of suburbs, grass-played sports, and gardened institutions. The global lawn-mower market in 2019 was valued at USD 28.5 billion, and the 2027 forecast is estimated at USD 44 billion.

Apparently, a little trimming can lead to great growth.

Printing Press and the Gutenberg Bible

Figure 5.2: A simple olive press and a coin punch inspired a device that produced the Gutenberg bibles and changed human history – the printing press.

Fusion(s): olive press and coin punch

Value: the spread of knowledge throughout the world and USD 6.3 billion (upper collective valuation) for the original 180 Gutenberg bibles

What on earth could a coin punch have to do with the olive-oil press? Certainly, coins printed with a standard punch could be traded for olive oil. However, the impact has been far more, thanks to a legendary inventor.

Johannes Gutenberg, a German merchant's son who lived in China for many years and grew up on a large agricultural estate, spent a lifetime observing wine and olive presses, as well as woodblock printing in China.

In about the year 1450, as an adult goldsmith, mold-maker, and inventor, he combined the flexibility of coin printing and mold-making with the olive press to create molded type-letters and a movable-type printing press. Before-hand, book pages were either hand-copied or pressed from woodblocks, at great expense and with much production time. With his invention, books could be mass-produced, and both knowledge and communication were revolutionized.

The first printed book he produced was the Christian bible – about 180 copies (see Figure 5.2). The current price of a complete edition is USD 25 to 35 million, making an upper valuation (if each edition were sold separately) of USD 6.3 billion.

Far beyond the value of these specific books, his invention led to the spread of knowledge throughout the world.

Value? Inestimable.

VELCRO®

Figure 5.3: Burdock and its clothing-catching hooks that inspired VELCRO®.

Fusion(s): Burrs and zippers; biology and mechanics

Value: USD 650 million

When electrical engineer George de Mestral went for a walk in the woods ad examined the small hooks on burdock seeds clinging to his trousers and his dog (see Figure 5.3), he was inspired to create a two-sided fastener, inspired by the zipper – one side with hooks and one with loops.

He patented the idea in 1955 and named the invention VELCRO®, for velour (velvet) and crochet (hook). He founded a company to produce and market the innovation, now valued at more than USD 650 million.

It is worthwhile, indeed, when faced with an innovation, to "stick to it."

Wheeled Luggage

Fusion(s): luggage and machine trolleys

Value: fastest-growing segment of the USD 21 billion luggage market, and many thankful travelers with bad backs!

Bernard Sadow was travelling through airport customs in Puerto Rico with his wife and kids wrestling with large, heavy suitcases, when he spotted a worker moving machinery on a wheeled platform. He told his wife they needed wheels on their luggage.

After developing and showing a prototype to every department store in New York (including Macy's), Sadow was refused by them all. In 1970, this former president and owner of a luggage company arranged a meeting with Macy's vice president, who accepted the idea and agreed to sell the product.

Sadow patented the invention two years later, but it was later overturned as the product became wildly successful. Nearly 20 years later, Sadow's wobbly coaster-wheeled, flexible-strap version was replaced by the retractable-handle suitcase, invented by Northwest Airlines pilot Bob Plath. His "rollaboard" suitcase launched the Travelpro® luggage company, and the basic design is still in use today.

The global luggage market is estimated at approximately USD 21 billion, and the casual bag segment (which includes wheeled bags) is the fastest-growing segment.

When innovating, it is important to "roll with it."

Wind-Up Radios

Fusion(s): clocks and radios (bot not as clock-radios)

Value: communication for 420 million people

More than 420 million people in Africa live in poverty – approximately one in three. Many have radios but no reliable electricity and no money to buy batteries. Sub-Saharan Africa is the global epicenter of human immunodeficiency virus (HIV)/acquired immunodeficiency syndrome (AIDS), and health information could be easily disseminated via radio – if they had power.

After watching a TV program describing the problem, Trevor Baylis created a solution within 30 minutes. He combined a radio with the wind-up mechanism of a traditional clock, making a wind-up radio.

Trevor was an engineer, physical trainer, stuntman, and inventor, who had left school at 15 without any qualifications. So many of his stunt friends suffered disabling injuries that he began inventing devices for them, including one-handed bottle openers and foot-operated can-openers, easels, and scissors – more than 200 inventions in all.

Sadly, no one was interested in producing the wind-up radio, so after Trevor's BBC World Service interview attracted an investor, he began manufacturing in South Africa with differently abled factory employees. Early versions were bought by aid agencies and given away, and eventually they became popular with consumers.

Baylis' design won the 1996 BBC Design Award for Best Product and Best Design and is now featured in the UK Science Museum as iconic British design and sustainable technology. Spin-off designs include electricity-generating shoes (enough to charge a mobile phone), a wind-up MP3 player, and a wind-up flashlight. It inspired large corporations to develop other eco- and cultural-friendly products. Baylis received both Order of the British Empire and Commander of the Order of the British Empire awards – the highest-ranking OBE, excluding knighthood/damehood.

Chapter 6
Healthcare

Figure 6.1: Combining cardio-vascular fitness, flexibility, and muscle strength set the stage for a world-wide fitness craze and the top-selling home-view video.

Aerobics and Jane Fonda's Workout: Integrated Fitness on the World's #1 Home Video

Fusion(s): strength and aerobic exercise; dance and gymnastics; exercise and home-use videos

Value: world-wide fitness movement and the top-selling home-view video

Exercise physiologist Dr. Kenneth Cooper and physical therapist Col. Pauline Potts were puzzled when some people in the US Air Force had good muscular strength but performed poorly at bicycling, long-distance running, and swimming. They experimented with patients using a bicycle ergometer and realized their trouble was in sustained performance activities that required efficient use of oxygen. In 1968, Dr. Cooper published *Aerobics*, which included exercise programs using bicycling, running, swimming, and walking.

https://doi.org/10.1515/9783110703009-006

A year later, Jacki Sorensen combined his work with dance and began spreading her new method of aerobic exercise – a fusion of dance and gymnastics – throughout the US via hundreds of new aerobics instructors (see Figure 6.1). Aerobics would ultimately combine dance, stretching, and strength training to impact all elements of fitness as an integrated health-enhancing whole – cardio-vascular fitness, flexibility, and muscle strength.

Just over a decade later, Jane Fonda integrated aerobic workouts with video production so people could exercise at home (mainly women – a new exercise audience). She produced *Workout* (also known as *Jane Fonda's Workout*), following her book and exercise record.

Workout was the top-selling VHS tape for six years, spread the practice of aerobics worldwide, set the standard for celebrity fitness, and funded Fonda's political activism (her original goal).

Her encouraging shouts of "Feel the burn!" and "No pain, no gain!" reverberate in exercise routines to this day – and political elections, too.

Aviation Healthcare at Rotterdam Eye Hospital

Fusion(s): aviation, design thinking, and healthcare

Value: 47 percent more patients at Rotterdam Eye Hospital, alongside improved speed and quality

---

Rotterdam Eye Hospital adopted innovations from the aviation industry in order to improve safety and service. These included "black box" recording, crew resource management training, patient planning and booking, risk analysis (to avoid wrong-site surgery), time-out procedures (also to avoid wrong-site surgery), and taxi service/valet parking. They also employed a design-thinking approach to their customer experience in order to turn a depressing, anonymous, and sterilized environment into a comforting, personal, and bright ambiance.

Awareness of patient safety increased, work processes standardized and improved in quality, waiting times reduced, wrong-site surgeries decreased, and patient intake rose 47 percent. They were nominated for the prestigious Dutch Design Award.

Apparently, aviation, design, and healthcare have something in common, after all.

Coca-Cola Medicine Delivery

Figure 6.2: A little empty space can save a life.

Fusion(s): FMCG distribution and medicine

Value: free delivery of life-saving anti-diarrhea kits, to save lives all over the world

---

As an aid worker in Zambia, Simon Berry saw a healthcare opportunity in an unlikely place – Coca-Cola crates (see Figure 6.2). He'd been working with child mortality, and one of the biggest killers is diarrhea – easily treatable with Oral Rehydration Solution, which is basically water, salt, and sugar.

Sound a bit like Coke?

Coca-Cola's distribution network covers 200 out of 202 nations on earth and was created in order to distribute a product that was originally a medical aid distributed via pharmacies. In fact, in some places, it's easier to get a Coke than clean water. Berry wondered how Coke manages to distribute beverages to remote areas while aid organizations and governments find it hard to distribute medicine.

Then again, why wonder why if you can harness the power of something that already works?

In 2008, Berry began the ColaLife campaign on Facebook, which gained the attention of the BBC and then The Coca-Cola Company itself. Thus began Cola-Life as a registered UK charity, collaborating with The Coca-Cola Company. They experimented with crate-side pouches and tubes that would replace a bottle, but both would introduce a cost to the beverage distributor.

Then Berry's wife suggested using the unused space in the crate. After nearly a dozen re-designs with their packaging partner, wedge-shaped anti-diarrhea kits are placed between the necks of crated cola bottles. The package is both a measuring cup and a storage container and introduces no additional cost.

As it turns out, Coca-Cola doesn't own their entire distribution chain – most particularly the "last mile." However, ColaLife has "piggybacked" on the journey to the wholesaler and priced its product reasonably, so the last-mile distributors can also earn a profit (introduced, of course, by their cola partner). Everyone wins, especially consumers.

What else might go well with a Coke and a smile?

Given Imaging: Guided-Missile Gastroenterology

Fusion(s): researchers from a variety of fields and nations; a host of technologies integrated into the wireless capsule endoscope; ideas and people

Value: USD 160 million annual revenues for 220,000 life-saving endoscopy capsules

---

Israeli Ministry of Defense (MoD) engineer Gavriel Iddan transformed the medical field of gastroenterology when he pioneered wireless capsule endoscopy. It all began when he took a sabbatical from the electro-optical design research and development (R&D) department at MoD–Rafael. He was interested in medical imaging and wanted to study X-ray and ultrasound technologies in Boston. His neighbor and friend, gastroenterologist Eitan Scapa, also took a sabbatical in Boston and shared ideas on fiber optics, which were useful in endoscopy but could not reach the small intestine.

Charge-coupled device (CCD) imaging chips became commercially available, and when Iddan went on sabbatical again 10 years later, he suggested letting the endoscopic device travel independently, via a mini-transmitter (somewhat similar to a guided missile). Unfortunately, it wasn't practical because (among other problems) the devices could only be powered for 10 minutes and couldn't produce enough imaging to be useful before running out of energy.

However, later, while reading a journal on optical engineering, Iddan learned about complementary metal oxide semiconductor (CMOS) technology that required only 1 percent of the energy of CCDs and were predicted to replace them. The author later assisted the multi-organizational, multi-disciplinary engineering team Iddan put together with Gavriel Meron, who raised funding and recruited talented physicists and engineers. Alongside continuing advances in component miniaturization, their combination of funding, team, and technology would prove fruitful.

Leading experts at Sarnoff Corporation predicted it would be impossible to generate sharp diagnostic images with CMOS technology, but one of the founding team members knew the engineers at Tower Semiconductor who had already solved the problem. (Apparently scientific advances are both technical and social in nature.)

This solution paved the way for Iddan and Meron to found the Given Imaging company in Israel in 1998. Soon after, the team joined forces with UK researchers they met at a conference (again, highlighting the productivity of technological and social integration). Four years later, the first international capsule endoscopy conference was held in Rome, Italy.

Capsule endoscopy is now a commercial life-saving technology. More than 2,500 peer-reviewed publications, as well as international conferences, have grown from a single dream: to combine a host of technologies in a way that could save lives.

After 20 years of development – from concept to Food and Drug Administration (FDA) clearance – annual sales have passed 220,000 capsules and nearly USD 160 million.

Whether a missile or a mission, our missives are guided.

Healthcare Games: The Children's MRI

Fusion(s): amusement-park-type fun and hospital diagnostics; children's museum training for healthcare workers; customer experience design and technology

Value: 90 percent higher patient satisfaction scores; anesthesia use down from 80 percent to 10 percent; benefits for hospital, patients, employees, and insurance providers; higher revenue, lower cost, and lower risk

---

Doug Dietz was a medical-equipment designer/technologist at General Electric (GE). One day, he was in a hospital looking at one of his magnetic resonance imaging (MRI) machines and was dismayed to see a little girl crying and terrified. He learned that 80 percent of the children who use the machine have to be sedated in order to use the machine. If the anesthesiologist is not available, families are told to come back tomorrow, and the ordeal continues.

Drawing from Design Thinking ideas, techniques, and process at Stanford's d.school, he began empathizing and learning about the patient's experience and designed a new one. No changes were needed to the underlying technology, but the results would be dramatic.

When a patient and parents/guardians enter the diagnostics room, they would see the walls and machine decorated as a pirate ship. The patient begins on a dock near a shipwreck and sandcastles in a corner, and healthcare workers (trained by children's museum staff who know how to entertain children) explain the game. After "walking the plank" into the machine, they were told, "Shhhh – be very still – you don't want the pirates to find you."

Now, only 10 percent of the children need to be sedated, patient satisfaction scores rose 90 percent, and Doug was happy to see one little girl tug on her mom's skirt and ask, "Can we come back tomorrow?" Patient care is safer without the risks of anesthesia, more children can use the machine each day, revenues are up, and workers are less stressed.

GE Healthcare has expanded the pirate theme into the Adventure Series, which includes:

– Coral City Adventure, including a disco ball that makes "light bubbles"
– The Yellow Submarine, in which kids listen to harps
– Cozy Camp, in which children use a special sleeping bag under a starry sky in a "campground"
– The Rocket Ship, where kids are asked to tell the technician when the rocket goes into "overdrive" – an otherwise scary boom the machine makes

Sometimes technology improves our human lives. Sometimes, humanity improves our technology.

Minute Clinics: Fast-Food Healthcare

Figure 6.3: The name says it all!

Fusion(s): inexpensive, fast-food-style service and healthcare

Value: affordable healthcare with little or no waiting time

The United States is touted as both the biggest fast-food market in the world, as well as the nation with the highest health-care costs (Harvard School of Public Health, 2020). Is it any wonder, then, that it would be the originator of fast-food -style healthcare (see Figure 6.3)?

The most successful of the genre is Minute Clinic (now owned by CVS Pharmacy, which makes prescription-filling highly convenient). It offers little or no waiting time (a relief to anyone who has spent hours in "emergency" waiting rooms), as well as 50 plus percent lower fees than private-care physicians – 75 percent cheaper than emergency rooms. Minute Clinics are open 24/7, when most physicians are not available, and an emergency room is the only other care option.

Staffed by nurses and/or physician-assistants, with a physician either on-site or on-call, Minute Clinic (and others in its healthcare category) offers only routine medical services, that is, treatment for conditions such as colds, rashes, ear infections, employment physicals, immunizations, sore throats, and bronchitis. Some locations offer drive-thru COVID-19 testing and other diagnostics.

Criticism abounds, but staff know their limits and refer more complicated conditions to physicians and hospitals. Patients also know their level of dissatisfaction with full-care hold times, waiting times, physician schedules booked weeks in advance, cost, and the frustrating experience of navigating all those challenges just to be told that your child does, indeed, have an ear infection, and after half a day wrestling the healthcare system, here's the prescription we gave you the last time he had an ear infection.

With hundreds of locations and many thousands of satisfied patients, it seems they feel their minutes are well spent.

NVIDIA: Gaming for Healthcare

Fusion(s): gaming and healthcare

Value: USD 323 billion

A pioneer in accelerated computing, chip-making, artificial intelligence, and the gaming industry (their first "killer app"), NVIDIA now uses their chips, graphics software, and simulation engines for healthcare, autonomous vehicles, and other simulations. They do more than run simulated car games. They test new drug therapies, train doctors in rare conditions, guide real Mercedes vehicles, and more.

If they had asked for approval beforehand to develop multi-million-dollar healthcare simulations for drug testing and medical-worker education, they would likely have been turned down and would not have found a user base willing to experiment with the software and improve the chips and simulation engines.

However, using an already-developed gaming simulator in other industries makes perfect sense.

Every industry they started in was – at the time – worth "zero billion dollars." Now the company, working in multiple industries, is worth USD 323 billion.

Ritalin: Psycho-Active Drugs for Kids

Fusion(s): drug and (later) diagnosis; science and social forces

Value: a top-50 most-prescribed medication in the US with 2.4 billion doses issued worldwide

Leandro Panizzon was a chemist working for CIBA (now Novartis Corporation) in 1944. His wife, Marguerite (nicknamed Rita), had low blood pressure, which interfered with her tennis game. To help (and to create something generally useful at work, we assume), he synthesized methylphenidate, a short-acting stimulant.

He named it Ritalin, after his wife.

After FDA approval in 1955, it was, indeed, useful for patients with depression, narcolepsy, and emerging from induced coma, as well as geriatric patients with fatigue and depression. Early adverts showed "before and after" imagery of elders and housewives, for example a grey-haired housewife facing a mountain of potatoes (before) and peeled potatoes alongside a Ritalin-treated, cheerier-looking lady (after).

Despite the stronger-than-coffee pep-pill marketing, it failed to become a best-seller.

In the 1960s, psychiatrists like Charles Bradley began using psychostimulants on "maladjusted children" to improve behavior and school performance, based on earlier studies at children's psychiatric institutions in the 1930s.

Why did it take 30 years for school performance, children's behavior, and psychostimulants to converge and attract attention? By the late 1950s, the US had entered the "Cold War," escalating concerns about American children's education.

With that context in mind, CIBA then had a new market to explore: underachieving schoolchildren. In 1962, the FDA approved their petition to market Ritalin for children.

It was an "overnight success."

Critics claim that CIBA marketed attention deficit hyperactivity disorder (ADHD), not just their treatment for it. It is worth noting, however, that the 1960s in the US was a time in which psychiatry became acceptable (if not fashionable), and a range of psychiatric drugs (not to mention recreational) became popular, including "Mother's Little Helper" (Valium). Drugs were increasingly prescribed for both parents and children.

In essence, Ritalin was a drug in search of a disorder and in search of the right environment in which to succeed. Medicalization (for example, ADHD codification and diagnosis) and treatment (for example, choice of Ritalin as standard treatment) is not a purely scientific phenomenon. It proceeds successfully out of the interaction of science/technology advances and socio-political changes.

Succeed it did. In 2017, more than 16 million prescriptions were written for Ritalin in the US alone, 47th on the list of most commonly prescribed medications in the US. In 2013, patients around the globe took an estimated 2.4 billion doses.

Rita's little helper has become many people's little helper.

Chapter 7
Leaders and Organizations

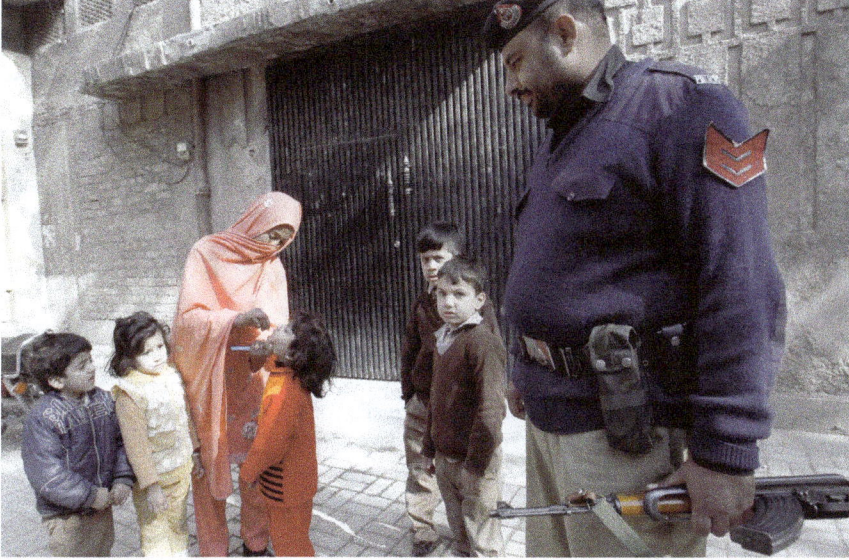

Figure 7.1: Polio eradication projects (like the vaccine dosing above) got a big boost when Bill Gates combined computers and emerging-economy vaccination.

Bill and Melinda Gates Foundation: High-Tech Humanitarianism

Fusion(s): high-tech and emerging-economy healthcare

Value: USD 14 billion by eradicating polio; lives saved and human wellbeing

---

One of Bill Gates' early and most passionate projects combined computers and emerging-economy healthcare (see Figure 7.1). Odd combination? Maybe not. Western administrators thought polio would be eradicated with the creation and distribution of the Salk vaccine. However, polio still proliferated in emerging economies.

By examining case data and combining it with geographical information, Bill and his colleagues discovered that new cases were arising at the borders between national/provincial/township and healthcare jurisdictions. Apparently, programs

https://doi.org/10.1515/9783110703009-007

worked well within their jurisdictions but not so well where borders were ill-defined and serviced.

Initiatives were put in place to eradicate polio at the borders, and now, polio cases number less than 40, worldwide. Apparently, polio eradication is expected to generate USD 14 billion of cost savings by 2050 when compared with the cost of controlling it indefinitely.

Lives saved, lifetime incomes earned, and elimination of healthcare programs all add up to billions of dollars of resources for future growth in economic progress and human wellbeing.

We are high-tech, and we are human, and we are growing through that synergy.

Elon Musk: Tesla and SpaceX

Fusion(s): Internet and business (software, then banking); aerospace manufacturing and transportation; cars, clean energy, and infrastructure development; friendly artificial intelligence; brain–computer interface

Value: richest man in the world with personal net worth USD 188 billion

Born of a Canadian mother and South African father, 10-year-old Musk learned computer programming via a user's manual and by the age of 12 sold a video-game he developed for USD 500. He was educated in South Africa and later, Canada and the US, receiving a dual bachelor's in economics and physics. He held two summer internships in the Silicon Valley – one at an energy storage start-up and the other at Rocket Science Games. The man who hired him – the former lead engineer for Apple Quick Time – remarked on Musk's boundless energy, background as a PC hacker, and proclivity to "go figure things out." Musk later moved to California to attend Stanford's Ph.D. program in applied physics and material sciences but instead of enrolling, decided to launch an Internet start-up.

He and his brother Kimbal co-founded Zip2, an Internet city guide (including contact information, directions, and maps) for the newspaper publishing industry. Since he couldn't afford an apartment or a second computer, Musk slept on the office couch, showered at the YMCA, and coded at night, seven days a week. They ultimately sold the company to Compaq for USD 307 million, of which Elon received USD 22 million. He then founded an online bank (X.com) that merged with Confinity (which had recently launched PayPal) and two years later was bought by eBay for USD 1.5 billion (of which Elon received USD 165 million).

Later that year, Musk founded SpaceX for aerospace manufacturing and transportation, in collaboration with the National Aeronautics and Space Administration (NASA), taking the roles of CEO and lead designer. He became the product architect and later the CEO for Tesla, an electric vehicle manufacturer. During that time, he helped create SolarCity, a solar energy services company, and later unveiled a concept for Hyperloop – a high-speed transportation system using pressurized capsules traveling on air cushion, driven by air compressors and linear induction motors.

He co-founded OpenAI, a not-for-profit research company promoting friendly artificial intelligence, and Neuralink, a neurotechnology company developing brain–computer interfaces. These high-tech enterprise foundings were followed by The Boring Company, an infrastructure and tunnel construction company crafting infrastructure optimized for electric vehicles. Most recently, he released an electronic dance music (EDM) track featuring his lyrics and voice.

Has this lover of business, engineering, design, manufacturing, music, physics, and programming been successful with his blending of diverse industries, fields, and technologies? Resoundingly, yes. *Forbes* magazine ranked him 25 in their 2018 list of The World's Most Powerful People, and jointly ranked him first in 2019's list of Most Innovative Leaders.

He is now the richest person in the world, with a net worth of more than USD 188 billion.

Lean Start-up and Open Innovation: Blending the Best of Start-ups and Mega-Corporations

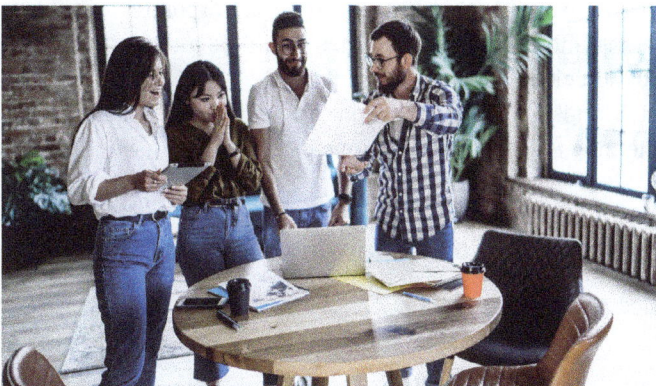

Figure 7.2: By combining forces (and methods), we can blend the best of small start-ups and big corporations.

Fusion(s): small start-ups and big corporations

Value: best-selling book and consulting sub-industry; partnerships between start-ups and big companies for innovation

---

Want to be a corporate-consultant guru? You could copy the career of *The Lean Startup* author, consultant, and coach. His book sold more than a million copies in 30 languages, listed on *The New York Times'* best seller's list, and launched a consulting field (see Figure 7.2).

Son of physicians and professors, sibling to a psychiatrist and a federal prosecutor, Eric Ries grew up in San Diego, where he's the only one at family gatherings without a master's degree or doctorate. Having studied philosophy and computer science at Yale, he dropped out to work at a start-up (which closed), finished his degree, then moved to Silicon Valley for another start-up (also closed).

He wrote about creating a "Minimum Viable Product," "pivoting" when your business needs a fast and radical change, staying close to customer needs, and more, all of which is now common language in both start-ups and corporations. Corporate executives realized his message wasn't just for start-ups looking to maintain their DNA as they scale – it was crucial to disruption-fearing corporates to regain their innovative DNA long after they had scaled.

In fact, for corporations that wanted to leverage the power of real start-ups (instead of only emulating them), the field of "open innovation" opened up, in which large and small firms collaborate to use the best of both, for example, nimble creativity and expertise of the small, combined with brand, customer base, distribution networks, and capital of the big.

Eric had no idea he would launch into a career of corporate consulting, coaching, and speaking and had no idea that his would be a new sector of an estimated USD 155 billion global consulting industry.

Apparently, small and big – and new and old – mix better than oil and water and have something to learn from everyone.

NetForm and TrustSphere: Social-Network Mathematics

Fusion(s): mathematical modeling, social systems, security, and human resources (HR); people and data

Value: one of the 100 most innovative companies in the world; a new field; and a multi-award-winning global company

---

Social Network Modeling as a field began as a combination of anthropology, field theory, and mathematical modeling. Later in its evolution, software development and management consulting ensued. Pioneer Dr. Karen Stephenson's journey began as a theorist in pattern recognition/mathematical modeling of networks and was one of the original thinkers that inspired this *Fusion* series. Her concepts were covered in best-selling book *The Tipping Point* and a 2000 *The New Yorker* article specifically on her work by Malcolm Gladwell.

CIO magazine rated Dr. Stephenson's company (NetForm) one of the 100 most innovative companies in the world.

As the social network analysis field grew, it spawned more companies, like premier firm TrustSphere. It began as a social-network analyzer looking at corporate email communication patterns to find malicious or unintended communications between staff and the "external" world (hence the name TrustSphere).

Soon afterwards, technology business leader and strategist Arun Sundar, who is also the founder of The Social Capital Institute, joined them. He brought his philosophy of Social Capital into TrustSphere. "Helping organizations understand social capital" became the mantra of the company, as well as "understanding people with data."

Moving away from security/risk-management, TrustSphere melded its methods and technologies with HR/people-analytics and sales analytics. It also expanded globally and grew its client base to include blue-chip companies like the world's leading French luxury brand, one of the world's largest consumer goods brands, and Asia's largest telecom conglomerate. It has won multiple awards for data management, analytics innovation, talent management, and online security, and became a Harvard Business School case study.

According to Stephenson, "a network *is* the structure of culture . . . as networks are resilient, held together by trust-based relations." Said another way, Warren Bennis describes trust as "the lubrication that makes it possible for organizations to work."

Apparently, understanding what trust is and how to manage it is good business.

Satellite Radio, United Therapeutics, and One of the World's Highest-Paid CEOs

---

Fusion(s): satellite and radio; multi-disciplinary healthcare innovation; technology, law, business, and much more

Value: USD 24 billion, USD 6 billion, and the highest-paid female CEO in the US

Leaving college half-way through would worry any parent. However, no worries were needed for Martine Rothblatt (formerly Martin). Her journey was exceptionally productive. Having traveled through Europe, Iran, Kenya, and Turkey, she had an epiphany in the Seychelles – to unite the world via satellite communication.

She finished school, ultimately earning an MBA and JD, and introduced satellite technology into a stodgy, dying industry – radio. Having extended and revitalized public transmissions, Siris Satellite Radio grew into Sirius XM Holdings (folding in other innovations and activities), now worth USD 24 billion.

Years later, Martine's daughter was diagnosed with a rare and fatal disorder. Without a medical degree or healthcare experience, Martine located a pharmaceutical company that had partially developed a drug to combat the illness. However, they had shelved it due to small market size and little hope of development success.

In a desperate attempt to save her daughter's life, Martine convinced the pharma company to license the "technology" to her, agreeing to pay them USD 25,000 and 10 percent of any future revenues she might receive. She soon found that it had a short half-life and no clear route to development.

Unfazed, Martine collected a multi-disciplinary team, developed the drug, saved her daughter's life, and saved many more lives with the drug that is now distributed by the company she founded, United Therapeutics.

She now pays USD 100 million/year in royalties to the licensor, and United Therapeutics is worth USD 6 billion. Martine became the highest-paid female CEO in the US, as well as the highest-paid biopharmaceutical-industry CEO.

Her interests, achievements, and career encompass astronomy, aviation (as an airplane and helicopter pilot and co-developer of the first full-sized electric helicopter), entrepreneurship, law, life sciences (including the Human Genome Project), lesbian, gay, bisexual, transgender, queer (or sometimes questioning), and others (LGBTQ+) rights, organ transplant technology, satellite engineering, space colonization, sustainable building, technological immortality (via mind uploading), transhumanist philosophy, writing, and vlogging.

She holds doctorates in law, medical ethics, and multiple honorary doctorates. She has worked with NASA and GeoSTAR and launched multiple technology companies, including the first international space-communication network (PanAmSat, which began as a school-project business plan), the first global satellite radio network (WorldSpace), and much more.

Forbes magazine listed her among the "100 Greatest Living Business Minds of the Century."

The Tiger Center: The Golden Triangle

Figure 7.3: Tigers, environment, and people must work together to survive and thrive. Photo source: Prof. Nishi Mukerji, The Tiger Center, Kanha National Park.

Fusion(s): economy and ecology; business and society; developed and developing economies; leadership team diversity

Value of India's tiger reserves: USD 230 billion of "green capital"; 4,600 more tigers, estimated at USD 10 billion in economic benefits per year; 200 to 530 times return on each dollar spent maintaining a tiger reserve

---

Once, more than 100,000 tigers roamed the earth. In 2008, only 1,400 remained in India (2,000 worldwide), and three sub-species were totally extinct (Ministry of Environment, Forest and Climate Change, Government of India, 2016). From the early 1900s until then, at least 93 percent of the tiger's range had been eradicated (Verma et al., 2017).

An unusual set of friends, family, and community banded together to do something about it. The original idea was to establish an education center and resort that would educate business leaders about economy and ecology, as well as raising money for guns and other equipment, personnel, and training to protect the endangered tigers living in the forest (see Figure 7.3).

However, when the founders discussed the idea with forest service officials, they were told they had the wrong problem. The service had plenty of people, training, and equipment, but guards can only do so much. The real guardian of the tiger and the forest is the community – the people who live around the tiger.

When we began our journey (yes, I am one of the founders), the community faced 75 percent unemployment; earned USD 1/day when they could get work; had to travel 60 km away (37 miles) if they needed medical assistance; and had no effective, formal education for their children until children were age 10.

While investigating problems and conditions, the founders went to the Sariska Nature Reserve in Rajasthan, India. Their pre-arranged Forest Service meetings were cancelled that day at the last minute because all the Sariska tigers (30) had disappeared overnight. Investigators went to the surrounding villages, and everyone they met said they had seen nothing. No poachers, nothing.

As anyone who has lived in a small town or village can tell you, everyone knows everyone's business. However, the people were not committed guardians of the tigers they lived with and had not fought off poachers. Indeed, tigers often come into conflict with people when they take a farmer's ox for food or when someone gathering grass or wood for a fire stumbles upon one that attacks because it was startled.

Man can be friend or foe – or silent witness and supplier.

The founding team realized the forest officials were right. For the tiger to survive and thrive, it needs a natural environment with enough food and other conditions for it to live well and reproduce. For the environment to thrive, the community around it cannot encroach upon the forest to build, collect honey, hunt, poach, and so on. For the people to thrive, they need to be able to earn a living and have resources at hand so they don't have to go into the forest. Further, if the community depends on the tiger and environment for their livelihood (for example, from ecotourism), they will guard it with their lives.

Thus, "The Golden Triangle" model of conservation was born – promoting endangered species, environment, and people, for the benefit of all. The model evolved over the years based on initiatives that had impact and synergy.

The founders set up a social enterprise to promote the welfare of tigers, environment, and people, in an integrated way, aimed at helping all of them survive and thrive together. Success is measured in terms of people, profit, and planet – what is more popularly known as the "triple bottom line," a concept that had been only recently popularized. In fact, social enterprise – a fusion of charity and business – was also a relatively new concept they had to explain to potential business partners.

Leadership emerged locally and globally, from France, India, Ireland, Italy, Singapore, the US, and the UK. Their professions include accountant, architect, artist, attorney, chef, designer, ecodevelopment consultant, entrepreneur, financier, government leader, naturalist, nun and educator, police commissioner, professor, strategist, technologist, translator, tribal leader, and village leader.

They began programs for people, which now include an art gallery; beekeeping; distribution of clothing, blankets, toys, and water filters; furniture factory; medical camps; snake removal; tailoring certification; and tribal cultural events. Employment, wages, and wellbeing have all increased.

The Golden Triangle model of "eco^{2}development" (the "2" signifying ecological and eco-nomic) was discussed in the Parliament of India and influenced public policy at national, state, and forest-service levels. Follow-on work was done in "green accounting" for the Supreme Court to establish the economic value of trees, which also guided public policy (Anand, 2021).

Today, if we assume the rate of increase continues from MOE 2016 figures (rounding upwards due to Mahapatra's higher 2019 growth rate), then in 2020, we can estimate roughly 6,000 tigers in India – an increase of 4,600. According to Bagla (2017) and Verma et al. (2017), each tiger's "flow benefit" (roughly, its economic impact) is approximately USD 2.2 million annually, making the increase worth more than USD 10 billion annually.

In fact, every dollar spent managing India's tiger reserves creates an estimated USD 200 to 530 dollars of economic benefit. Verma et al. (2017) estimated that out of India's 50+ tiger reserves, conserving six of them (including Kanha National Park) is the equivalent of maintaining USD 230 billion worth of monetary capital.

That said, there are two elements generally missing from the economic studies. They already include oxygen, timber, micronutrients, and other elements but neglect the impact on income and employment for the people living around the reserves. Further, beyond economic calculations lie the intrinsic worth of this endangered species, its irreplaceable environment, and the wellbeing of thousands of people who visit and live alongside them.

The success of The Golden Triangle model locally – and its influence across India – provides us with an important underlying lesson: synergy. Beyond specific programs that aim to create one benefit, we can create integrated initiatives that achieve far more impact because they use the underlying synergies already inherent in the problem.

In L. Frank Baum's classic story *The Wonderful Wizard of Oz,* Dorothy and her friends calmed their nerves on the way to Emerald City with the phrase, "Lions, tigers, and bears, oh my!" The story was actually an allegory for youth, industry, farmers, and a famous political orator on the way to visit the president in Washington, D.C. Each one wanted something, helped others, and then discovered he or she had the object of desire already.

Perhaps we already have what we want, too, and just need to take care of it: tigers, environment, and people – oh my!

Chapter 8
Science

Figure 8.1: Merging elements from different scientific fields is one way to "evolve" a new one.

Albert Einstein: Energy and Mass, Space and Time

> "If I were not a physicist, I would probably be a musician.
> I often think in music. I live my daydreams in music.
> I see my life in terms of music . . .
> I get most joy in life out of music."
> – Albert Einstein

Fusion(s): energy and mass; space and time; philosophy and science

Value: foundation of modern physics

Albert Einstein famously worked at a patent office early in his career, while searching for a teaching position. Much of his work there focused on electro-mechanical signals and time. Although tempting to declare patent-office work as beneath the capabilities of one of the greatest geniuses the world has ever seen, his work there did apparently influence his thought experiments that led to his work on the nature of light and the connection between space and time (see Figure 8.1).

Having connected space and time, he crafted theory to support what would later become known as the theory of relativity – the most famous physics theory, foundational to modern physics. He also created the "world's most famous equation," $E = mc^2$. Similar to space and time, he saw a connection between energy and mass and created theory and mathematics to support that connection.

https://doi.org/10.1515/9783110703009-008

Did mathematics and physics consume all his thoughts? Apparently not. He is also known for his work on the philosophy of science and was an exceptional violinist.

Charles Darwin: Theory of Evolution

Fusion(s): natural history, biology, and geology

Value: inestimable – new scientific theory (evolution)

Born to a wealthy doctor and financier named Robert Darwin, young Charles Darwin was sent to the University of Edinburgh Medical School to follow in his father's footsteps. Unfortunately, Charles found the lectures boring and surgery stressful, so he spent his time in other pursuits. He learned taxidermy from a freed slave, joined a natural-history debate society, studied marine invertebrates, and learned geology and biological plant classification.

His father was not impressed. Robert promptly transferred his son to Christ's College, Cambridge, where Charles was to earn a Bachelor of Arts degree on his way to becoming a parson. Charles read materials on the role of God in the workings of nature, which built on the natural history debates he had joined earlier. He eagerly took part in naturalist and geological field studies with his classmates.

Post-graduation, Charles was offered a spot on the HMS *Beagle* as a self-funded gentleman scientist. Although Robert initially objected to that now-famous journey, he ultimately agreed to fund the trip.

During that historic, nearly-five-year journey, Charles collected specimens, kept copious notes and journals, theorized, and ultimately returned to England, where he was already a scientific celebrity, thanks to publication of his letters. Robert organized investments for his son, who then permanently became a self-funded gentleman-scientist.

Six months after returning home, Charles integrated his deep understanding of natural history; long-term perspective gleaned from geology studies; and biological observations across a variety of species and environments, most notably coral–colony life cycles.

In the same way that spotlights from three different directions highlight an actor on stage, three perspectives highlighted a new insight – species may not be permanently distinct but may, indeed, transform from one into another.

He recorded his speculations in one of his notebooks and began his work on the Theory of Evolution. The idea would make him one of the most famous scientists in the world and spark religious and scientific debate for nearly two centuries.

There is no way to estimate the value of this particular scientific theory. However, it has made an undeniably grand impact on science, religion, and society, and clearly required the integration of his diverse background and different perspectives.

We do not currently have evidence of the "missing link" between apes and humans. However, we do have evidence via Charles Darwin's life and work that different perspectives and fields can integrate and evolve into an idea, then into theory, and then into impact. Perhaps ultimately that is a more important evolution that we can all engage in.

Leonardo da Vinci: Art, Science, and Modern Acoustic Theory

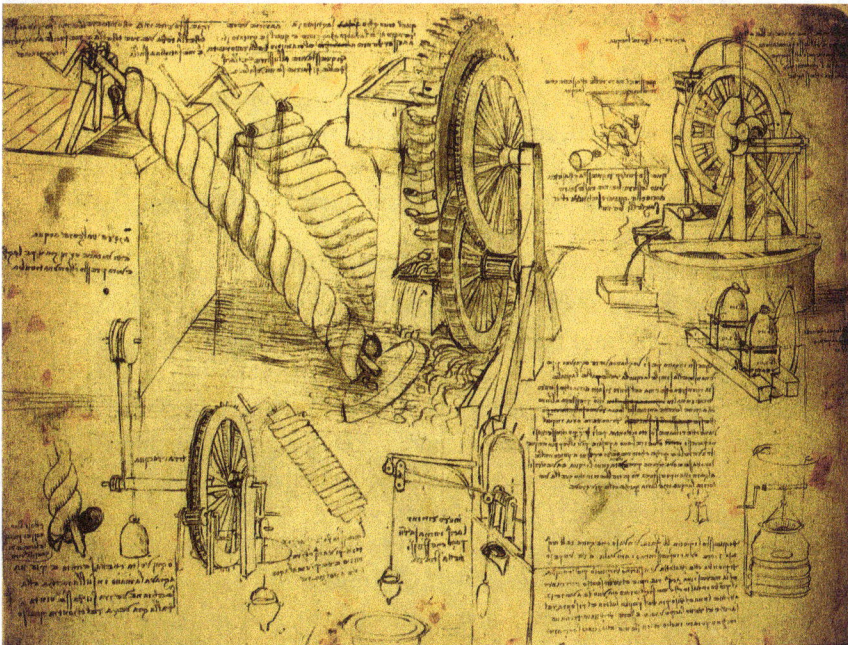

Figure 8.2: Quintessential Renaissance-man da Vinci integrated art, science, and engineering/inventing to excel at them all.

"Study the science of art. Study the art of science. Develop your
senses – especially learn how to see. Realize that everything
connects to everything else."
– Leonardo da Vinci

Fusion(s): art, science, and inventing; sight and sound resulting in modern acoustic theory

Value: highest insurance value in the world on the most famous portrait ever made (*Mona Lisa*, USD 850 million); highest painting value sold at auction (USD 450 million); a new field (modern acoustics); art, inventions, and more

---

As the illegitimate son of a notary and a peasant, young Leonardo could not be admitted to any school for formal education. Instead, he studied Latin, geometry, and mathematics informally and became a studio assistant for painters and sculptors. In these studios, he learned both theory and practical skills such as drafting, drawing, chemistry, leather-work, mechanics, metallurgy, modeling, painting, plaster casting, sculpting, and wood-work. He later lived with the Medici and worked among the world's finest artists, poets, and philosophers, sponsored and brought together by that famous family during (and resulting in) the Italian Renaissance.

His scientific studies of perspective and light had a profound effect on his artwork (see Figure 8.2). Deep and detailed understanding of anatomy, botany, geology, light, and the physical expression of emotion enabled artistic creations that were second to none. Self-education and diversity of interests fostered an ability to see the world in a unique way.

Although initially famous as a painter, he was later recognized for the inventions and scientific work in his notebooks, which included the fields above plus astronomy, cartography, and paleontology. He envisioned and designed an adding machine, the double hull, flying machines (including the helicopter), the parachute, solar power, and the tank. Most of his creations were so advanced they could not be produced successfully with the science and technology of his time. Indeed, his advances in anatomy, civil engineering, geology, hydrodynamics, optics, and tribology were unpublished, so had little influence on those fields at the time.

However, there is a theory he is well-recognized for – modern acoustical theory – resulting from a fusion of sight and sound. He was walking by a pond one day and saw ripples in the water at the same time as hearing a church bell. He connected the sight and sound and theorized that perhaps sound travels in waves. The rest is theoretical history.

Famously, his letter to the Duke of Milan offering his services detailed the advances he could make for the Duke in engineering and weaponry and mentioned in passing that he could paint.

Heralded as the best example of a "Renaissance Man," with unquenchable curiosity and intense imagination, many consider him to be one of the (if not the) most diversely and deeply talented people who ever lived.

His most famous painting and the most famous portrait ever made – the *Mona Lisa* – holds the highest-ever insurance value for a painting at USD 850 million. His *The Last Supper* is the most reproduced religious painting in the world. His portrait of Jesus (*Salvator Mundi*) sold at auction in 2017 for USD 450 million, the highest price ever paid for an auctioned painting.

Gregor Mendel: Mathematics + Biology = Genetics

Fusion(s): statistics/mathematics and biology

Value: USD 22 billion genetic testing industry and related industries

Moravian monk, mathematician, biologist, and meteorologist Gregor Mendel founded a scientific field – genetics – by combining mathematics and biology. He carefully cross-bred peas, tested hypotheses of inheritance, and made statistical predictions and mathematical models of trait inheritance before genes themselves were discovered. His work established the laws of heredity and concepts such as dominant and recessive inheritance.

Mendel and his family valued education but had few resources to pay for it. Although monkhood was not his original vision, Mendel brought his significant talents in physics and mathematics to the Augustinian monks, who valued education, research, and science. He joined the order and later continued his education at the University of Vienna, where, despite his shy nature, he discovered a talent for teaching.

Mendel did not aim to create a new scientific field. He just wanted to create hybrid pea plants and observe the outcome. However, given his methodical nature, hypotheses that led to further questions and hypotheses, detailed record-keeping, and bias for experimentation, he established the principles of a new field and was the first to use statistical methods to analyze and predict hereditary traits.

Although his work was published, it was ahead of its time, and the significance was not fully appreciated until after his death. He was elected abbot of his parish and became a political activist toward the end of his life.

Nearly a century and a half later, genetic testing alone is predicted to be a USD 22 billion industry by 2024 (Medgaget, 2021). When genetic engineering and related fields are added in, the value is substantial.

Apparently, math and biology belong together – like two peas in a pod.

Chapter 9
Services

Figure 9.1: Making something private (sex) public launched a whole new field – media psychology.

Commerce Bank: Fast-Food Financial Services

Fusion(s): banking and fast-food

Value: USD 8.5 billion company

Vernon Hill, a fast-food franchiser, melded banking and fast-food into Commerce Bank. Like his fast-food restaurants, his bank was open 24/7 and sported the motto, "No Stupid Fees, No Stupid Hours." He offered a penny-arcade machine that counted coins for customers and non-customers alike, gave lollipops and dog biscuits at the drive-through window, and issued pencils, pens, and mugs in the style of children's-meal toys.

Was it successful? Well, TD Bank purchased Commerce Bank for USD 8.5 billion.

We don't know if they got fries with that.

https://doi.org/10.1515/9783110703009-009

Dr. Ruth: Sex (Therapy) on the Radio

Fusion(s): private and public

Value: a new field (media psychology) and a revolution in how a nation (or the world) talked about something basic to our human experience: sex

---

What's the most private, not-talked-about topic you can think of? Sex would be high on the list for most people.

What's the most public forum in 1980? There were two – radio and TV (see Figure 9.1).

So who would talk about sex on the radio?

Dr. Ruth Westheimer began her sex-therapy-popular-media career in a forum no one else on her school's faculty wanted – radio. She lectured to New York broadcasters on the need for sex education to reduce unwanted pregnancies and to promote contraception. NYNY-FM picked up the idea, offered her USD 25/week, and broadcast her show *Sexually Speaking* in a 15-minute timeslot, aired on Sunday at midnight.

Three years later, it was the top-rated ratio show in New York (despite the odd timing), and the following year, NBC syndicated it nationwide as *The Dr. Ruth Show.*

The hit show continued until 1990, during which time she revolutionized how the nation talked about sex and engaged in public-forum sex therapy (hitherto unknown). Dr. Ruth was candid, funny, helpful, informative, serious, and had a voice one journalist described as a cross between "Henry Kissinger and Minnie Mouse" (Schuessler, 2012).

In 1984, she began hosting TV shows, including *Good Sex! With Dr. Ruth Westheimer, The Dr. Ruth Show, Ask Dr. Ruth, The All New Dr. Ruth Show, What's Up, Dr. Ruth?,* and *You're on the Air with Dr. Ruth.*

"Dr. Ruth" became a household name in the 1980s, and she made guest appearances with Johnny Carson, David Letterman, *Hollywood Squares, The Today Show,* Ellen DeGeneres, Seth Meyers, and more, as well as a host of other TV shows and commercials. She inspired a PBS wildlife series for children, an off-Broadway play, and a well-acclaimed 2019 documentary.

She taught at Princeton and Yale, received honorary degrees, gave commencement speeches internationally, and received a medal for her humanitarian work, not the least of which is with child refugees. She understands the pain they experience, as a German-American holocaust orphan.

She speaks English, French, German, and Hebrew, is a trained military sniper, and has authored 45 books during her 92-year lifetime. After being transferred to a Swiss orphanage when her parents were taken during the Holocaust, she made friends with a boy who – unlike her – was allowed to study in high school and lent her his school materials. The dormitories were strictly lights-out at night, so she sat in the stairwell with borrowed books to read and learn.

Vanity Fair named her one of "12 women who changed the way we look at sex" and said that with her clinical training and "sassy attitude [she created] the first widespread outlet for anonymous, prompt, trust-worthy sex advice" (Berliet, 2009).

Some say she created the field of media psychology. Some say she revolutionized sex therapy. Most who consulted her say she created human wellness – one person (or couple) at a time.

Eat Purr Love: Cat Cafés/Dog Cafés and Animal Therapy

Figure 9.2: Combining coffee and cats (or dogs, dolphins, horses, donkeys, pigs, and so on) saves pet lives and enhances human wellbeing.

Fusion(s): cafés and pet adoption; animals and "sterile" environments

Value: lives saved and wellbeing enhanced via thousands of pet adoptions and animal-therapy encounters worldwide

---

What do you get when you cross a cat with a cup of coffee? Something much better than hairy coffee (see Figure 9.2).

Cat cafés began in Taiwan, and there are now more than 100 of them in the US, plus many more around the world. Dog cafés joined the fold, and there are additional cafés that focus on pigs, hedgehogs, and more.

Eat Purr Love in the US reports more than 550 adoptions in their first four years of operation, after launching via a Kickstarter crowd-funding campaign. Animals in the home-like café are more relaxed and show their personalities far better than in traditional animal-shelter stacked cages. Patrons mix and mingle with multiple animals, get to know them, and form bonds that often result in adoption but sometimes results in a form of pet-therapy for customers who cannot adopt pets due to family fur allergies, unfriendly landlords, and so on.

Eat Purr Love went a paw-step further and added special events including Yogatos (yoga with a *gato* – Spanish for cat – on your mat), Kids and Kitties (kids' and cats' story-time), cat-themed movie night, and Purrs and Palettes (for wine and painting).

In fact, the field of pet therapy has grown remarkably in recent years. Many hospitals, pediatric-care facilities, schools, special-needs programs, nursing homes, and other facilities that had prided themselves on their "sterile" environments that excluded animals now welcome pet therapists and host animal-assisted intervention programs. Animals in-service include dogs, cats, dolphins, horses, donkeys, pigs, and many more. Research abounds on the positive effects for all concerned, and the field continues to grow.

Fast-Food Weddings at A Little White Chapel

Fusion(s): fast-food and weddings

Value: 50,000 marriages (no, I'll not speculate on the value of that or how many of them are still together)

What began as a way for differently abled couples to marry – with one or both partners in a wheelchair, using a walker, sporting a cane, and so on – became something much more: Las Vegas' most iconic chapel. Not only did differently abled couples love the new service, but couples enjoying the US fast-food culture enjoyed it as well, whether from the US or abroad.

More than 50,000 drive-through weddings have been performed at A Little White Chapel in the past 30 years, including the likes of Britney Spears, Bruce Willis, Frank Sinatra, Judy Collins, and Michael Jordan.

Las Vegas wedding tourism topped USD 2.5 billion in 2018, and A Little White Chapel is its champion, having hosted hundreds of thousands of weddings outside the drive-through. For more than 68 years, the chapel's owner has hosted weddings 365 days a year and provided her famous one-stop-shopping model – an integrated service for wedding ceremonies, gowns, flowers, tuxedos, and more, making elopement easy.

If only the marriages were that easy. But that's another story.

FedEx: An Envelope in Every (Airline) Seat

> "The mind generates creative ideas by making connections between
> seemingly unrelated variables. The creative impulse rests on
> seeing new possibilities and new combinations. For the
> mind to generate creative ideas, it must either connect
> existing dots (one's knowledge base) in new ways
> or acquire and connect new dots."
> – Madan Birla, *FedEx Delivers: How the World's Leading Shipping*
> *Company Keeps Innovating and Outperforming the Competition*

Fusion(s): postal delivery and air travel; creative capabilities of all employees in an innovative culture that developed new services and grew the company

Value: USD 66 billion company

Yale University. 1965. Student Frederick Smith wrote that although airlines would occasionally carry time-sensitive cargo such as documents, computer parts, electronics, and medicines, the routes were not optimized for urgent shipments (thus slower than necessary), and the customer journey was not optimized, since packages had to be delivered to and picked up from an airport. Fred's paper proposed a system designed for efficient delivery by night, when passenger airport traffic is reduced.

No one paid attention.

In 1971, Fred developed his idea into a business plan for the world's first company dedicated to overnight package delivery and launched the business in 1973. It took two years to earn its first profits. It earned, and it grew. In 1978, FedEx was listed on the New York Stock Exchange (NYSE), and in 1983 was the first company to reach USD 1 billion in revenues within 10 years without acquisitions. In 1984, it began international operations.

Recognized as one of the best companies to work for in the US and one of the Most Admired Companies in the US (by *Fortune* magazine), FedEx grew not only out of an initial fusion by the founder (document/package delivery and airline travel) but by continual service development by employees integrated with one another in an innovative culture.

FedEx now delivers more than 5 million packages a day to 215 countries and has market capitalization of more than USD 66 billion.

It didn't absolutely have to be there. But thanks to the vision of one man and the creative efforts of many, it is.

Harvard Business School: The Case Method

Figure 9.3: Combining the topic of business with the pedagogy of medicine and law produced one of the finest schools in the world.

Fusion(s): pedagogy from law and medicine applied to business

Value: 113-year-old business school with a USD 3.5 billion endowment

---

When the Harvard Business School was founded in 1908, the Industrial Revolution was in full swing, and business enterprises were growing at a seemingly uncontrollable rate. Railroads were being built and administered, as well as steel mills, coal mines, textiles, and more.

A new breed of manager was necessary – one to handle large enterprises, not just village general stores. Ideas and frameworks were borrowed from the military, but there had to be a way to teach new business managers so they would be well-prepared to assume their posts (see Figure 9.3).

There were no textbooks for industrial-age business, since business grew ahead of academic visioning and training. Law and medicine had long used the case method to prepare professionals via applicable theory and – importantly – practice.

The new school adopted the methods of law and medicine, and theory grew as the golden age of industrial management developed. However, the pioneer in management education did not turn its back on practicum. As a practical discipline (like law and medicine), management students would need theory but would need to continue the case method in order to hone not only theoretical skills but also practical.

Thus began what I believe (yes, indeed, I am biased) the finest management education – immersion in theory, decisions in-practice, and reflection on wisdom.

When they decided to offer an advanced degree beyond the MBA, it was the DBA – Doctorate in Business Administration – not a PhD – Doctorate in Philosophy. In the same way that an MD is different from a medical PhD and a JD (juris doctorate) is different from a PhD in law, every practitioner is different from a theoretician, but integrating theory and practice has proven valuable in business (witness the rise of consulting), law (ask any supreme-court judge), and medicine (ask any doctor who has gained an insight from patients and researched it for many more).

If it weren't valuable, it wouldn't last.

IDEO and Design Thinking: Design, Technology, and Business

Fusion(s): design and other fields; design, technology, and business; desirability, feasibility, and viability

Value: 2X industry growth, 60 percent more shareholder returns, and more

Every field has its own way of thinking and communicating – expert methodologies, tools and techniques, professional language, and industry jargon. In 1987, Harvard Professor of Architecture and Urban Design Peter Rowe described how architects and urban planners think and create in the course of their work and uncovered the underlying thought-and-creation characteristics common to a variety of design fields.

These thinking processes inspired others to apply what then became known more generally as "design thinking" (DT) outside of design fields – to business product development, business and government service development, employee experience, social enterprise, and more.

The top design consultancy in the world is IDEO, which has methodologies old and new and created iconic products such as the first commercially viable computer mouse, four hours of government service delivered in 10 minutes, global food innovation via the Rockefeller Foundation, the *Free Willy* movie whale, and much more. The largest digital and design-thinking consultancy in the world is iX, at IBM. The Stanford d.school, at which IDEO founder David Kelley teaches, has its own methodology, as do many others.

According to IDEO CEO Tim Brown (Brown, n.d.), what is common to all of design thinking is innovation at the intersection of:
– desirability (what people need and want)
– feasibility (what is now technologically possible) and
– viability (a sound economic way to provide it)

Methodologies begin with user-empathy and problem-discovery, proceed to out-of-the-box solution-development, and then prototype and experiment before moving on to detailed development and launch.

Does it create value? Resoundingly, yes. According to a variety of research studies, the value includes:
– business-growth double the industry benchmark and up to 75 percent more returns to shareholders by top design-index companies (Sheppard et al., 2018)
– three times operating income growth, two times return on assets, and up to 60 percent more shareholder returns by companies who directly capture customer insights (as DT practitioners do) (Jaruzelski, Staack, and Goehle, 2014)
– financial "outperformance" by companies that drive growth seeking new needs (as DT does), as opposed to those that drive growth by "market reading" or "new-tech investing" (Jaruzelski, Staack, and Goehle, 2014)
– outperforming peers by 231 percent (Westcott et al., 2013)
– outperforming the Standard and Poor (S&P) by 228 percent (Westcott et al., 2013)

DT is useful for "wicked" problems, where we don't know the solution and, in fact, don't really know the problem either. It is a critical methodology for complex situations and human-centered difficulties, which characterizes many of humanity's most-pressing problems today. How can we design better ways of living?

It isn't true that if you build it, they will come. It is true that if they want to come, you should probably build it.

Legal Grounds: The Law-Firm Coffee Shop

Figure 9.4: Coffee with law and justice.

Fusion(s): lawyer's office and coffee shop

Value: comfort and justice

Who wants to meet up with a lawyer, with bad coffee in a sterile, expensive office? What's the opposite? Meeting up with friends in a coffee shop afterwards?

Why not combine the two?

That's exactly what David Musslewhite and his wife did (see Figure 9.4). Located in a Dallas shopping center, you can slip into Legal Grounds and as easily talk to an attorney as you would your best friend. Apparently, latte blends well with legal, and the café offers "murderous mocha" as well as "equal-rights espresso."

A simple legal intervention is also on the menu, and the ambiance is littered with volumes of legal statutes and overstuffed chairs. David the lawyer and his wife the café chef split their time in the café, legal office, and mopping the floor, which endears their clients beyond anything they could parade as lawyer and chef.

Justice must be tempered with mercy to be truly just. And a cup of coffee wouldn't hurt.

StockX: A Stock Market for Sneakers (and More)

Fusion(s): sneakers and the stock market

Value: USD 1 billion business

Josh Luber had a lifelong fascination with sport shoes and start-ups. He earned his law and business degrees at Emory University, founded two companies, one of which was an IT services firm he successfully built and sold.

After joining IBM in New York, he again worked on his own projects after-hours. One of them (Campless) tracked resale prices on eBay – the first database of its kind – with a crowdsourced staff of contributors. He regularly worked on it until 4:00 am and then clocked in at IBM at 9:00 am.

About 600 miles away, billionaire Dan Gilbert, co-founder of Quicken Loans and owner of the Cleveland Cavaliers, noticed that his teenage sons were spending a lot of time on eBay, bidding on sneakers. He discussed it with Greg Schwartz, who had founded a calendar app with Gilbert's investment funding. They believed a "stock market of things" was a winning idea and believed that not only should the first featured products be sneakers, but a "sneakerhead" should lead it.

After flying Luber out to a Cavaliers game, they listened to Luber explain his ideas of a sneaker stock market and a price guide that would incentivize buyers to create sneaker portfolios. The three of them collaborated non-stop, Luber wore the same clothes for three days, returned home to his very pregnant wife at 1:00 am, and said, "I think we're moving to Detroit."

Three days later, he was a father again (second child), and the three men gave birth to a new company. Gilbert and Schwartz bought Campless and within two months launched StockX with their new partner.

Part Amazon, part eBay, part traditional stock exchange, StockX is a platform for trading collectible handbags, sneakers, streetwear, trinkets, and watches, in a double-auction format that allows buyers to place maximum bids and sellers to place minimum offers. When the two match, the transaction is executed, and StockX earns a commission of 9.5 to 14.5 percent. The sneaker and streetwear retail market in North America is valued at USD 2 billion, estimated to be USD 6 billion by 2025, and their ultimate vision is to host a stock market of things.

Four years later (in 2019), StockX brokered more than USD 1 billion of sales.

Unlike Amazon and eBay, the platform maintains a single listing page for every sneaker model, and authenticators scrutinize products in more than a dozen ways (yes, including the smell test) to verify their legitimacy. "Certified by StockX" is now a coveted authentication (with its own imitators), and sneaker portfolios are managed similarly to stock portfolios.

Original products are now developed for and sold exclusively on the platform in initial product offerings (IPOs) (similar to the stock market's initial public offering of company stocks). There are even derivatives and other stock-market-style transactions.

With 1,000 employees and all the complications of a growing corporation, Luber handed over the CEO title to Scott Cutler, who helped grow eBay, StubHub, and the New York Stock Exchange. Luber develops new lines of business (for example, baseball cards) and new creative ideas.

StockX has been valued at more than USD 1 billion. With persistence, hard work, and a winning idea, success can sneak up on you.

Subway: Healthy Fast-Food

Fusion(s): healthy food and fast food

Value: USD 10.4 billion annual revenue (2019); largest single-brand restaurant chain and largest restaurant operator in the world

---

Who would predict that Doctor's Associates Inc. would own one of the world's top fast-food companies? Isn't fast-food bad for you?

Not necessarily. Also, the brand didn't begin as an affront to unhealthy fast-food.

In 1965, in order to earn enough for medical school tuition, Fred DeLuca borrowed $1,000 from his friend Peter Buck (who had a doctorate in physics) to start "Pete's Super Submarines." The following year, they founded Doctor's Associates Inc. to oversee operations and expansion. The company didn't begin with a vision to "Eat Fresh" (a later motto) or a health campaign, but it did evolve in that direction.

Healthy fast-food was on its way.

By 2010, Subway became the world's largest fast-food chain – with 1,000 more outlets than McDonald's. In 2015, it was ranked the fastest-growing franchise and a top three global franchise. Eager for constant improvement, the business modernized with USB ports at tables and gluten-free bread, but it faced market pressure and falling sales in the face of consumer desire for hormone-free meats and locally sourced produce.

Nonetheless, Subway today comprises more than 44,000 outlets world-wide across 100 countries. Privately owned by the DeLuca family, it has 30,000 employees and is the world's-largest single-brand restaurant chain, as well as the world's-largest restaurant operator.

Sounds like not really a sub-way but rather a super-way, to eat and do business.

Chapter 10
Technology

Figure 10.1: Combining art and technology can, indeed, make our hearts sing.

Apple: The Art of Technology

> "Technology alone is not enough. It's technology married with
> the liberal arts, married with the humanities, that yields
> us the results that make our hearts sing."
> – Steve Jobs

Fusion(s): art and technology

Value: USE 1.95 trillion company; world's most valuable brand (USD 241 billion per Forbes ranking, Swant, 2020); revolutionary changes in four industries: computing, music, publishing, and telecommunications

---

No writing on high-value creativity and innovation would be complete without at least a mention of Steve Jobs and Apple (see Figure 10.1). (For more information on Pixar, see "Disney and Pixar: The Technology and Business of Art" above.)

Steve dropped in on a calligraphy class in college before dropping out to travel India and learn Zen Buddhism. He later credited that class for inspiring Apple's beautiful typography. His spiritual wanderings and artistic nature seem to have similarly inspired the beautiful industrial/technological designs for which he and Apple became famous.

Steve Jobs and Bill Gates became icons of the personal-computer revolution that changed the world. Essential to that revolution was the graphical user

https://doi.org/10.1515/9783110703009-010

interface (GUI), which made computing more accessible and appealing to consumers than mere logic, 0s and 1s, and symbolic programming languages that dominated the computer industry beforehand.

Steve saw great potential in the mouse-driven GUI, as well as laser-printed vector graphics (introduced with the Apple LaserWriter) and desktop publishing (pioneered with the Apple Macintosh). He later invested in Lucasfilm's graphic animation division, which became Pixar and produced the world's first three-dimensional computer-animated feature film (*Toy Story*).

Everything Steve produced was visually beautiful and composed with elegantly designed simplicity, be it a personal computer (from Macintosh to MacBook and iPad), music devices and system (iPod and iTunes), desktop publishing (iStudio), or the mobile phone (iPhone).

Hybridizing art and technology, logic and creativity, the graphic and symbolic, has, indeed, led to much good fruit.

Atari and *Pong*: Personal Arcade Games

Fusion(s): games and mass-market electronics

Value: USD 162 billion (global gaming industry); first commercially viable video game; USD 143 million (Atari)

Nolan Bushnell was an incessant game-player – *Monopoly*, *Clue*, chess, and especially *Go*, a conceptually simple game from Japan with infinite board configurations. He was equally consumed with electronics and science, ultimately studying electrical engineering in college, where he first encountered the computer game *Spacewar!* It was love at first sight, and he was fascinated by the impact it had on his fellow students, who lavished their time on the game instead of their studies.

Nolan worked his way through school at an amusement park, where he happily parted patrons with their money for the chance to play games. Nolan envisioned the day pinball games would be replaced by electronic fun like *Spacewar!*

However, that day would not come quickly, since the mainframe computer that hosted the game cost USD 120,000. He later encountered games on minicomputer, but the USD 40,000 price of the machine still made it commercially inviable for mass-market use.

Nonetheless, he and fellow-engineer Ted Dabney turned a bedroom into a computer lab and searched for a way to commercialize computer games. They realized that instead of using more advanced technologies like the mini-computer, they could do the reverse – simplify their game design and use transistor-to-transistor logic (TTL) to create a single-use device.

With USD 100 of electronics and a TV, they created the first commercially viable video game, called *Computer Space.*

For the next five years, all video games used Nolan's discreet-logic technology. The engineering approach was very much like the game *Go* – simple, but with infinite possibilities. Unfortunately, the game itself was not. It was too complex, so lacked consumer appeal. They needed a game that (like *Go*) was "simple to learn, difficult to master."

While trying to sell *Computer Space*, Nolan happened on an analog-computer game developed for Magnavox. It had fuzzy graphics and could only support very simple play. However, the tennis game he watched stuck with him and became the origin of the ping-pong game he would develop – *Pong.*

Nolan and Ted formed a company in 1972, and Nolan suggested the name Atari, which in the game of *Go*, means, "Watch out – I'm about to win." The logo was a triangle that could be an "A" but actually looked more like Mount Fuji.

Nolan set to work designing a new game, and Ted launched a coin-operated game service. Nolan hired an engineer and set him to work on *Pong* as practice toward a full-feature commercial game. However, they discovered that the simple ping-pong play was a lot of fun, and when they introduced it as a coin-operated game in arcades and bars, it was a runaway success.

Patrons would go to bars just to play *Pong* without ordering any drinks, and the machines jammed when coins were stuffed into the receiving slots in a desperate attempt to play, despite the coin bins being full.

By the following year, Atari had earned more than USD 3 million but attracted the attention of two key players. First, before a patent could be awarded (a three-year process at the time), new competitors sprung up and copied the simple TTL design, which had chips instead of a microprocessor and could easily be taken apart and replicated. By the end of the year, Atari was no longer *Pong's* leading manufacturer.

Second, Magnavox demanded a licensing fee, since the idea came from them.

Cleverly, Atari paid Magnavox USD 500,000 before going to court and specified in the agreement that Magnavox and its excellent legal team would pursue all the copycat competitors.

Atari was free to move forward and develop other games.

In fact, they not only created more arcade games but found a way to put *Pong* on a single chip, which meant they could develop the home-gaming market – dual-game-industry leadership no other company had yet achieved.

The rest, as they say, is history, except for one little-known episode worth noting. *Pong's* engineer, Allan Alcorn, hired a young wiring technician – Steve Jobs – and an engineer for Atari's coin-op *Breakout* game – Steve Wozniak. The two Steves were friends, and after the first Steve moved on to HP, they crafted (in their garage) a new computer based on the same processor Atari was using for coin-operated games. Al liked the machine but thought Atari was the wrong fit to promote it and introduced the two Steves to some venture capitalists.

That was the Apple I, and the rest is Apple history. Atari regretted letting it go when entering the home computing market a few years later.

However, Nolan never regretted a life of games and electronics. He used technology to solve problems and was fascinated with Disney, which used technology to entertain. Although he didn't invent video gaming, he did commercialize it and set an entire industry in motion.

Given the size of the industry and the size of the company, perhaps a better translation for *Atari* is, "Watch out – we're about to win."

Google: Academic Citation Rankings for All

Fusion(s): academic citation ranking applied to webpages

Value: USD 1.38 trillion company; second most-valuable brand in the world (USD 207 billion per Forbes ranking, Swant, 2020); most-visited website in the world (and owner of two more – YouTube and Blogger)

Stanford University. 1996. PhD students Larry Page and Sergey Brin were working on a research project and saw a connection between academics and the Internet. Since academic articles are likely to be more important the more they are cited, shouldn't there be a similar way to rank and search web pages?

Early search tools like Archie, Veronica, Gopher, and eventually Yahoo! did not operate that way. They were closer to manually created library catalogues than genuine search engines. Web search was nowhere as easy as it is today, and any form of manual cataloguing would predictably inhibit the Internet's usefulness as a communal information medium.

So, Larry and Sergey crafted their entirely automated PageRank algorithm. Instead of counting how many times a search term was repeated on a particular page, their algorithm assessed the relevance of a website to the search by assessing the number of pages in the site and their importance to the search, including not only the search terms but potentially also timeliness, authority, and novelty.

The search engine was nicknamed "BackRub" because it checked back-links but then was changed to Google, an intentional misspelling of googol (1 followed by 100 zeroes), to indicate that the engine could process a great deal of information.

A host (not quite a googol) of new services, partnerships, and acquisitions were integrated into the company following the original search engine, including advertising, artificial intelligence, cloud storage and computing, communications, email, electronics, hardware, mapping and navigation, media and videos, publishing, scheduling tools, shared documents, software, translation, virtual reality, and more.

Google has now even gifted itself to the world by being verbed ("I'll google that.")

Apparently, academic exercises can offer practical use. I wonder how often Google itself has been googled . . .

Litterati and Plogging: Ecofriendly Social Media

Figure 10.2: Plogging combines exercise and eco-action and can be posted on technology platform Litterati.

Fusion(s): sustainability and social media; exercise, technology, and trash (pick-up); individuals acting together for impact

Value: global trash-clean-up movement and a new sport – plogging, which boasts events with more than 3 million participants

Nearly 40 million photographs are Instagrammed each day. (In fact, the company name is now a colloquial verb.) Not only are friends and family "hashtagged" with the posts, but food (traditionally a communal experience) figures heavily, including #food (more than 134 million posts), #foodporn (more than 32 million posts), and more.

Since 49 percent of litter is food packaging and food waste, tech-entrepreneur Jeff Kirschner decided to connect food waste and social media. By 2013, he founded Litterati to crowd-source litter disposal, growing a social movement in the process (see Figure 10.2). Basically, when an Instagrammer (now a colloquial noun) sees litter, he or she can photograph and Instagram it with #litterati, pick it up, and place it in a trash or recycling bin.

Geotagging and interactive maps document the impact, and Kirschner partnered with the California Coastal Commission, Levi Strauss & Co., the National Resources Defense Council, and Whole Foods to promote Instagram competitions (not yet a colloquial phrase), offering prizes and freebies.

Where did the idea come from? He was hiking with his kids when his four-year-old daughter pointed to a plastic tub, and he remembered a practice from when he was a child at summer camp. Once each child had picked up five pieces of trash on "Visiting Day," the camp would be clean. If children can do this on a small scale with their hands, he wondered what everyone could do on a global scale with their hands and phones.

In about 2016, an organized activity began in Sweden that combined jogging with picking up litter, giving not only eco-significance to jogging, but also integrating it with bending, stretching, and squatting. In both Swedish and English, the activity was named an integration of two words, hence the term "plogging."

More than 20,000 people are estimated to plog each day across 100 countries, and plogging events have been held with more than 3 million participants. Litterati offers a way to share both organized plogging and casual litter collection. In its first two years of operation, nearly 73,000 photos across 40+ countries included the fast-trending #litterati hashtag.

Individually, we make a difference. Together, we make an impact.

Microsoft Office: Integrated Words, Numbers, Graphics, and Communication

---

Fusion(s): words, pictures, numbers, and email

Value: USD 20 billion annual revenues

Before Word, there were WordPerfect and WordStar. Before PowerPoint, there was Harvard Graphics. Before Excel there was VisiCalc. Before Outlook, there was Lotus Notes.

Were MS Word, PowerPoint, Excel, and Outlook each better than their competitors?

Actually, no. Most advanced users of the software recognized that the specialists offered more features and were in some ways superior at what they did.

So why am I not typing this book on WordPerfect or WordStar?

Because the Microsoft Office suite did something they didn't – seamlessly integrate words, pictures, numbers, and communication in ways that users found easy. People want to create and communicate verbally, numerically, and graphically, using and mixing whatever media is appropriate for a particular idea at a particular moment.

So the integrated solution took over the market from the specialists, and I'm using MS Office to prepare this book for you.

NASA: The Hubble Telescope's Shower-Head Mirrors

Fusion(s): space telescope and shower head

Value: USD 4.7 billion

NASA's Hubble Space Telescope cost USD 4.7 billion when it launched and had a small problem: it couldn't focus. It needed small, coin-shaped mirrors to reflect light from a particular location. Unfortunately, scientists could envision no way to deliver and insert them.

While adjusting his shower head, Space Telescope Science Institute's Head of Programs James Crocker realized that a similar approach could solve NASA's 4.7-billion-dollar problem. By extending the mirrors (inside a replacement axial device) into the light via remote control using articulated arms similar to a shower head, the telescope could finally produce clear scientifically useful images.

How's that for a clean solution?

Pokémon Go and *ARQuake*: Outdoor Augmented-Reality Gaming

Fusion(s): virtual-fantasy gaming and real-life action

Value: USD 21 billion market capitalization growth (Nintendo); USD 6 billion revenues (*Pokémon Go*); first outdoor augmented reality (AR) game (*ARQuake*)

Co-developed by Niantic, Nintendo, and The Pokémon Company, *Pokémon Go* became *the* global gaming phenomenon of 2016, with more than 500 million downloads by the end of the year, 1 billion downloads by early 2019, and more than USD 6 billion revenue by the end of 2020. Nintendo's market capitalization more than doubled to USD 42 billion – in just seven stock-trading sessions post-*Pokémon*-launch.

The game uses augmented reality (AR) and Global Positioning System (GPS) to provide players with the chance to find, fight, capture, and train virtual *Pokémon* characters that appear in real-world physical locations. It encourages gamers to engage in outdoor physical activity (a revolution in gaming) and has benefited local businesses via increased foot traffic. Unfortunately, in some cases crowding became a public nuisance, and accidents ensued as gamers paid more attention to the virtual world than the physical dangers around them.

Although by far the most popular outdoor AR game, it was not the first. University of South Australia's Wearable Computer Lab created *ARQuake* in the year 2000, an AR mod (version) of id Software's game *Quake*. With a head-mounted display and tracker, GPS, handheld shooting device, and a UNIX laptop on a special backpack device, gamers traversed the real and virtual worlds in search of virtual monsters.

Sadly, the 16kg (35 lb) gaming device didn't gain mass popularity the way *Pokémon Go* did, operating from a light mobile phone its users carried anyway. However, it did pave the way forward into a combined virtual and physical world.

Who knows where *Pokémon* and gamers will "Go" next?

SpaceX: Rocket Recycling

Figure 10.3: Space meets sustainability in rocket-booster recycling.

Fusion(s): space and sustainability (recycling and rocket boosters)

Value: USD 1.16 billion

Rocket boosters hold fuel and, once spent, have traditionally been ejected, only to fall to earth and land somewhere in the ocean – single-use devices. Elon Musk's SpaceX company, however, has combined space and sustainability in a way that takes recycling to a whole new level (see Figure 10. 3).

At SpaceX, the booster detaches from the rocket when the fuel is spent and then lands right-side-up on a platform, to be reused in 20 to 30 future launches. SpaceX has landed boosters 58 times and re-used them in 40 launches.

At USD 20 million per booster, that means they've saved USD 1.16 billion so far.

With sustainability like that, perhaps we won't need to relocate to other worlds.

WWW: Connecting Computers, Information, and Humanity

Fusion(s): business, computers, culture, information, people, and more

Value: USD 2.1 trillion to US gross domestic product (GDP) (but in total, inestimable)

The ultimate form of collecting-the-dots and connecting-the-dots would have to be the Internet (or World Wide Web) itself. Its origins date back to the 1950s, when computers were extremely expensive, and researchers wanted to both collaborate and time-share their machines. International connections and wide-area-networks soon arose.

In the 1960s, two researchers independently conceived of (a) distributed networks operating on message blocks and (b) commercial data networks operating on packet switching – a form of data blocks. The United States Department of Defense's Advanced Research Projects Agency (ARPA) used the approach and built ARPANET.

More networks followed, and protocols were proposed for inter-networking separate networks (making a network of networks). In 1974, researchers at ARPA and Stanford laid the foundation for what would become the Internet's Transmission Control Protocol (TCP) and Internet Protocol (IP).

The Doman Name System evolved in the 1980s, followed by the work of British computer scientist Sir Timothy Berners-Lee, who linked hypertext documents, accessible from any node in the network, which became known as the World Wide Web. He created the first web browser, as well as the algorithms and protocols that enabled "The Web" to scale.

In the mid-1990s, the Web grew beyond research into a general communication and commercial platform, impacting business, culture, and technology. Its growth and adoption have been phenomenal.

In 1993, only 1 percent of two-way-telecommunicated information was hosted by the Internet. In 2007, 97 percent flowed over the Internet, thanks to the advent of discussion forums, email, instant messaging, online shopping, social networking, video chat, and voice-over-Internet.

The Web is now infused in our economies and lives in a way that makes it difficult (or impossible) to estimate its impact and worth. However, the Internet Association has tried and has estimated in 2019 that it was worth USD 2.1 trillion to US GDP (that is, 10 percent of GDP), grew nine times faster than the economy as a whole (2012 to 2018), accounted for 4 percent of US employment, and created six million jobs in 2018. It supported another 13 million jobs indirectly, across all sectors of the economy. Within a decade, it quadrupled in size and became the fourth-largest industry in the United States.

The advent of Big Data and artificial intelligence systems with access to a world of current and historical information suggests that the Web is now a platform for something beyond connected ideas and people. With the work of people like Rick Smolan, *Time*, *Life* and *National Geographic* photographer, publisher, and co-author of *The Human Face of Big Data* (2012), we now must contemplate that connected information and communication is evolving into emergent intelligence.

It's a debate for another day where the Web will lead us, or where we will lead it. For now, we witness its miraculous growth and all that we collect and connect with it.

> "'What's miraculous about a spider's web?' said Mrs. Arable.
> 'I don't see why you say a web is a miracle – it's just a web.''
> Ever try to spin one?' asked Dr. Dorian."
> – E.B. White, *Charlotte's Web*

Chapter 11
Travel and Housing

Figure 11.1: Through repeated re-launch and re-design, the Airbnb founding team created the world's most successful integration of private homes and Internet booking.

Airbnb: Internet Home-Hotels

Fusion(s): Internet booking platform, private homes, and a traditionally real-estate-intensive industry (hospitality)

Value: USD 118 billion company

Rent is very expensive in San Francisco – how can anyone afford it? Even having roommates, it's hard to cover the rent. I know – why not put an air mattress in the loft, serve breakfast, and call ourselves a bed-and-breakfast?

Sounds a mildly unappealing idea, but that's just what two roommates and former design-school chums did – Joe Gebbia and Brian Chesky – to raise money for rent they couldn't afford (see Figure 11.1). They knew an important design conference would be held soon, and hotel rooms would fill up. Would anyone be willing to sleep on someone's floor for a chance to go to the conference? In fact, if they could be tour guides as well then it might be a fun way to make money.

https://doi.org/10.1515/9783110703009-011

They built a site called airbedandbreakfast.com, put three air mattresses in their loft, and – *ta-da* – were open for business. After a few happy customers, they invited their old roommate, Nathan Blecharczyk, to help them turn it into a business.

Since home-hotels were such an unlikely idea (unless registered as bed-and-breakfast businesses), they developed a roommate-matching service for four months. Unfortunately, they found roomates.com had already launched.

They launched again, and no one came.

Then they launched again and had one customer.

They redesigned so rentals could be booked in three clicks and asked investors to help. Eight angel investors turned them down. Seven didn't respond. Although vacation rentals by private landlords had been done online before Airbnb, most of the rentals were investment properties, and many were professionally managed – more appealing than an air mattress and toast.

They thought back to their first success and realized when hotels were all booked up, people would consider alternatives like theirs.

So, broke and in debt, they went to Denver. The 2008 Democratic National Convention was happening. To raise money, they created limited-edition cereal boxes called Obama O's and Cap'n McCain's, selling them on the street for USD 40 each. They netted USD 3,000, and each box included information about their new company.

One venture capitalist (VC) – Paul Graham – was intrigued and invited them to join the now-famous Y Combinator accelerator, providing cash and training in exchange for a small stake in the new venture.

They refined their business plans, stayed with hosts, photographed, leveraged their design backgrounds to feature hosts favorably on their website, and shortened the name to Airbnb. Sequoia Capital offered USD 600,000 of seed capital, and the business took off.

Four years after hosting their first air-mattress guest (and after four launches), they had booked 1 million stay-nights across 89 countries, attracted more VC money, and were valued at USD 1 billion.

Scale-up problems ensued, including lodging-trashing guests, complaining neighbors, city governments trying to legislate them out of their jurisdiction, and more. Nonetheless, they resolved issues as they came up and survived.

Airbnb is a prime example of Dr. Clayton Christensen's theory of disruptive strategy, in which new companies that shake up an industry don't enter from the top and offer superior products. They enter from the bottom. They either serve customers who are paying too much for what they really want, or who are not served at all – like conference-attendees in cities with booked-up hotel rooms.

Customers will turn to alternatives when they currently have no alternative. That's the big opportunity.

Today, the company is valued at USD 118 billion, owns no real estate (are they "just air?"), and has integrated additional services into the core business, such as excursions and activities, last-minute hotel bookings, premium services, and optimizing new apartment buildings.

So, whether the company is "just air" or not, it's apparently getting Better 'n Better.

BillionBricks: Architecture, Finance, and ICT for the Homeless

---

Fusion(s): high-end architecture, energy, finance, and information- and communications-technologies for economic growth

Value: four times energy-production than a family needs; potential housing for 1.6 billion people

---

According to the United Nations, 150 million people around the globe are homeless, alongside another 1.6 billion in inadequate housing. The catchphrase of COVID-19 has been "work from home." But what if you have no home?

After designing approximately 10,000 high-end homes, architect, interior designer, and urban planner Prasoon Kumar quit his profession and teamed up with entrepreneur and venture capitalist Anurag Srivastava to found BillionBricks. They created an innovation studio to build the world's first solar-powered tented community where poor residents can micro-finance their own homes.

Their first creation was an emergency tent that can protect from the cold or, when reversed, protect from heat and sun. One of the first recipients shared that it was her "first-ever home." From then on, Prasoon realized he wasn't just designing emergency shelter. He was designing homes.

Produced for a post-riot emergency in India and manufactured in China for designers in Singapore, these USD 300 tents have been distributed to Canada, India, Mexico, Nepal, and the US, and orders are arriving from funders around the world. Beyond homes, they are proving to be good bathrooms, changing rooms, shops, and phone-charging spaces.

However, BillionBricks is not stopping with tents. They are developing a permanent-construction, self-financing, carbon-negative solar home. Their homes are designed to produce four times the energy the inhabitants need. Thus, residents have electricity and can sell energy back to "the grid" to pay for the home.

Further, with rainwater collection, waste cleaning, and a front yard for growing food, housing becomes sustainable. Once Internet-connectivity is installed, remote work, online business, global communication, and economic growth become possible.

Then everyone can "work from home."

Prototypes have been built in India and the Philippines, and plans are in place for a 500-home community, with a vision toward 25,000 in the next five years. Foundational goals for the community – housing, education, food, healthcare, and work – in a scalable model that can be used around the globe.

Is it a housing development or an energy company?

Does it matter?

Boeing-NASA-Airbus: Manta-Ray Aircraft

Figure 11.2: Swimming manta rays are helping us fly better.

Fusion(s): manta rays and aircraft; swimming and flying (fluodynamics and aerodynamics)

Value: USD 16 billion; 183 million tons of CO_2 emissions

Although birds have been our traditional inspiration for aircraft, the aeronautics industry is now looking beyond aerodynamic inspiration toward the sea, for fluodynamic inspiration – most notably, manta rays (see Figure 11.2). NASA,

Boeing, and Airbus are working on a manta-ray-styled aircraft that could cut fuel use and carbon emissions by 20 percent.

Since the global airline industry's fuel consumption is estimated at USD 78 billion in 2021, that would mean a savings of nearly USD 16 billion if all aircraft were manta-designed. With 915 million tons of CO_2 produced in 2019, that would mean savings of 183 million tons of CO_2 emissions.

Whether we swim or fly, we still inhabit the same planet. Can we swim and fly better together?

Ford and Oldsmobile: Automobiles and Meat-Packing

Fusion(s): automobile manufacturing and meat packing methods; flow assembly, division of labor, and interchangeable parts; product- and process-design; wages and productivity

Value: USD 2 trillion (global automotive industry)

By the year 1104, the Italian city of Venice had constructed a complex of ship-yards and armories along a canal called the Venetian Arsenal. Ships would float down the canal, and the shops along the way would fit, arm, and provision a new ship in a manner similar to a modern assembly line.

By the early 1500s, the state-owned Venetian Arsenal – one of the world's earliest large-scale industrial operations – employed 16,000 people and could produce nearly a ship a day. However, without the technological and logistical conditions that fostered the Industrial Revolution (roughly 1760–1840), the method didn't make its way into other industries.

Across the globe, pre-Industrial-Revolution state-run manufacturers in China practiced division of labor before the Europeans, employing different workers for different production tasks. Adam Smith wrote about such division of labor in *The Wealth of Nations* (1776).

Nonetheless, before the Industrial Revolution, goods were produced mainly by craft, that is, by individual craftsman fashioning an entire product from start to finish. Eventually (1853), a method called "flow assembly" – similar to the Venetian Arsenal, but on a smaller scale – was used in the UK to manufacture portable steam engines.

The idea found its way to the US, and in 1901, Ransom Olds built the first mass-produced car, the Oldsmobile Model R (or Curved Dash). Olds added inter-changeable parts to the flow assembly, labor was divided among different stations, and he patented the assembly-line concept.

Years later (and allegedly independently), William "Pa" Klann at the Ford Motor Company visited a Chicago slaughterhouse and was intrigued with the "disassembly line," in which meat traveled from worker to worker, each removing a particular cut for packing. The meat packing industry in the US had been using the technique since 1867. He introduced the concept to Henry Ford, and in 1913, Ford Motor Co. used the assembly line to produce the Model T.

> "Henry Ford is generally regarded as the father of mass production. He was not. He was the sponsor of it."   – Charles E. Sorensen, *My Forty Years with Ford*

Ford reduced total assembly time from 12.5 labor-hours to just over 1.5. Cars were produced quicker than colored paint could dry, and only "Japan black" would dry fast enough. So, Henry is credited with another quotable quote:

> "Consumers can have any color of car they want, just so long as it's black."
> – Henry Ford (before fast-drying colors were developed in 1926)

Ford also increased wages, commensurate with workers' increase in productivity. When asked why he paid his workers so much, Ford famously replied, "If I don't pay them more, how can they afford to buy my cars?" This not only benefited workers but grew the company and the industry overall – and eventually changed the nation.

> "The assembly line technique was an integral part of the diffusion of the automobile into American society. Decreased costs of production allowed the cost of the Model T to fall within the budget of the American middle class. . . . In 1914, an assembly line worker could buy a Model T with four months' pay."   – Wikipedia

High productivity and wages became known as "Fordism" and became the accepted practice in many other industries, fueling overall economic growth. In addition, managers realized that when new products were designed, the manufacturing process also had to be designed, giving rise to integrated product- and process-design (or "design for manufacturability"). When World War II erupted, fast production of military hardware and armaments became a key capability for survival and victory:

> "We won because we smothered the enemy in an avalanche of production, the like of which he had never seen, nor dreamed possible."
> – William Knudsen, National Defense Advisory Commission,
> formerly at Ford and General Motors

So, although Ford did not invent the assembly line and was not even the first to use its concepts in automotive manufacturing, he did recognize the importance of it and the integration of production and consumption in our economic system. He understood that both sides must benefit in synergy, in order to grow.

In the face of today's arguably winner-take-all economics, with rising wealth and income inequality, and concerns over employment in the face of artificial intelligence and robotics, is this a lesson we need to re-learn?

What future will *we* craft? I don't know for sure, but I assume it'll be more colorful and diverse than monochrome black.

GPS: Taking Global-and-Local to a Whole New Level

Fusion(s): military and civilian; global and local

Value: USD 1.4 trillion; USD 1 billion per day if unavailable

Global Positioning System (GPS), a satellite-based radio navigation system, was built by the US Department of Defense from 1973 to 1993. It is owned by the US government, maintained by the US Space Force, and free for all to use (although originally restricted to US military use).

Modern GPS receivers (circa 2018) can provide a location within 30 cm (12 in), and organizations and individuals have devised a wide range of creative uses for GPS. For example, consumers use it for automotive navigation; getting transportation (for example, via Grab, Ola, or Uber); hobbies and sports (for example, geocaching, geodashing, GPS Art, and outdoor virtual games like *Pokémon Go*); photographic geotagging; travel and tourism (for example, accessing historical information in-context, on-location); and tracking (for example, people, pets, and certain electronics).

More commercial use includes aircraft and automotive location (for example, accident siting, logistics and fleet tracking, and self-driving cars); agriculture; astronomical, atmospheric, weather, and other scientific studies; cartography; communications (for example, in rural areas or disaster-relief and emergency services); clock synchronization; data mining; mineral mining; land surveying; robotics; and wildlife tracking.

The US government can restrict or degrade GPS service and, indeed, did so during the 1999 Kargil War. For this reason, other governments have developed or are developing similar systems.

However, government restrictions are today unlikely, since the National Institute of Standards and Technology estimates that losing GPS service would now cost the US economy an estimated USD 1 billion a day. They've calculated the economic benefits of GPS at USD 1.4 trillion since it was opened for civilian use in the 1980s.

Perhaps we've now answered the decades-old question, "What did we ever get out of the multi-billion-dollar space race?"

By traveling where no man had gone before, now we know where we are.

Heatwave: The Beautiful Radiator

Figure 11.3: Gallery art or radiator?

Fusion(s): design (art) and heat radiation (science); form and function; traditional and contemporary; natural and industrial

Value: beautiful warmth and a successful design practice and heating company

---

Most people have seen a radiator – normally an ugly object placed in sadly obtrusive locations to provide heat to a room. Some are more stylish, that is, partially hidden in baseboards.

However, Joris Laarman took a 180-degree turn and made radiators as art objects (see Figure 11.3). The designer's final thesis at the Design Academy in Eindhoven included the two-column Rococo radiator, first produced in 1895. Heat radiation is more efficient with more surface area, hence the traditional Rococo surface filigree. Laarman's new design takes the concept much further, combining functional efficiency with ornamental playfulness.

Using a classical filigree design with four interlocking pieces, the tips and curls of Heatwave suggest the movement of heat waves, effectively combining stasis and motion. With a flower-shaped control valve, an exuberant design reminiscent of swirling windblown autumn leaves, fashioned in an internally piped polyconcrete shell, it also integrates natural and industrial. The pieces can be assembled in a variety of ways to create both warmth and ambiance appropriate to the room's design – even curling around a corner for efficient space usage and artistic effect.

He continues to innovate at Joris Laarman Labs, and the Heatwave is sold by Jaga Climate Systems.

Can we be warm inside and out? Intellect and body? Apparently, yes.

Termite-Human Habitation

Fusion(s): termite mounds and architecture

Value: 90 percent energy savings on air conditioning – USD millions per building per year

In 1991, an investment group in Harare, Zimbabwe hired Mick Pearce to design the largest office and retail building in the country – Eastgate Centre – a 350,000 square-foot mega-complex. However, they didn't want to pay a huge price for air conditioning.

Mick looked to termite mounds for inspiration (biomimicry). He found that these cleverly built natural complexes can hold millions of insects in linked-mounds that can reach 5 meters high (16 feet). They include a multitude of small and large air vents above ground to release warm air, as well as substantial construction below-ground that absorbs and stores cool temperatures at night.

Based on these concepts and more, Mick used brick and concrete materials on the outer surface of the building to absorb heat while maintaining the interior temperature. With small windows, overhangs, and a cactus-style "prickly" exterior, heat gain is minimized during the day, warm air is vented and released by multiple chimneys in the roof, and heat loss continues during the night. Low-power fans pull in and disperse cool night air throughout the building, and concrete absorbs and holds the night-cold.

Despite the desire of the investors to minimize ongoing cooling costs, is air conditioning the right design focus? Is it really such a bad thing?

Lee Kuan Yew famously introduced air conditioning into Singapore's civil service buildings and declared,

> "[Air conditioning] changed the nature of civilization by making development possible in the tropics. . . . The first thing I did upon becoming prime minister was to install air-conditioners in buildings where the civil service worked. This was key to public efficiency."
> – Lee Kuan Yew, Singapore's first prime minister

One study supported that assertion by showing that in South-East Asia, people without cooling lost 15 to 20 percent of their productive work hours. In the Caribbean and Central America, every degree above 26 °C (79 °F) reduced GDP by 1 percent. Even in cool Boston, cognitive tests of students with air conditioning were higher than those without, and studies in Denmark showed higher math and language learning in air-conditioned schools, over those without.

Our global population is ageing and, thus, more vulnerable to heat stroke. French reform to install air conditioning in nursing homes is credited with saving thousands of lives. With urbanization, offices and factories are larger than ever and must be kept at a productive temperature for humans and machines. Hospital machines, vaccines, computers, and more require cool temperatures. Almost 25 percent of liquid vaccines spoil without proper temperature control, and health workers often don't know which vials are spoiled when they administer them.

Further, cooled storage and transport could offset the greenhouse-gas emissions from wasted agricultural production, half of which is lost in developing countries to insects and rodents. Each year, 600 million people become ill and 400,000 die from contaminated food.

Unfortunately, air conditioning warms the planet overall while cooling specific people and things. In Riyadh, 70 percent of peak-hour electricity demand goes to air conditioning, and Saudi Arabia is predicted to use more energy for cooling in 2030 than it now exports in oil. One research study has revealed that improving air conditioners and repairing their harmful-gas leakages could be our most powerful weapon against greenhouse gasses. India, for example, would save three times the carbon emissions as the Prime Minister's plan to install 100 gigawatts of solar power.

So, apparently, cooling is good and current air-conditioning technology (as used – chemical leaks and all) is bad. Thankfully, Eastgate shows us a model for the future. It uses 35 percent less energy than other office/residential buildings in the nation and 90 percent less than the building next door – all with natural design.

Cool, huh?

Uber: Internet Taxis

Fusion(s): GPS, Internet, and transportation; public transportation and private cars

Value: USD 75 billion company; USD 8 billion IPO (one of the 10 largest, ever)

What's one of the first things parents teach their children? "Don't get into a car with a stranger!" So what could be stranger than starting a new venture in which people get into strangers' cars?

Uber's origins are somewhat murky with Silicon-Valley lore. According to one account, the idea crystallized in a 2008 Paris snowstorm when the founders could not find a taxi. Another version states that a USD 800 New Year's Eve car hire inspired the idea in 2000. My personal favorite is that Uber started as a short message service (SMS) after major events like concerts, conferences, and sports games, when a sudden on-rush of people meant that many couldn't get taxis.

It was a fusion of public transportation and private car-hires. People could call an Uber dispatcher (similar to a taxi dispatcher), who would source a driver with a private car, and SMS the car number to the customer. Like Airbnb, which offered private accommodation when hotels were fully booked, Uber offered private rides when taxis were fully booked.

However the idea came about, it launched as UberCab in 2009 in San Francisco, and the app officially launched the following year. The app connected customers to premium-service black town cars at 1.5 times the price of a taxi. Predictably, city government (the first of many) ordered it to close down, due to the lack of taxi licensing, meters, and so forth.

Two days later, the company renamed itself Uber and continued operations.

In 2012 in Chicago, Uber expanded the app to booking regular taxis, as well. Soon after, UberX was added so customers could hail non-luxury rides (including personal cars), subject to background checks, inspection, insurance, and so on.

Customers loved Uber; taxis hated them; and cities had a problem on their hands with increased traffic, complaints citing regulations written before the age of the Internet, and more.

Nonetheless, Uber grew. In 2019, they had provided 7 billion rides across 69 nations (Kovaleski, 2020), boasting 65 percent market share for ride-hailing. Services expanded beyond ride-hailing to food and package delivery, courier services, freight, carpooling, and rental of electric bicycles and scooters.

The company raised more than USD 8 billion in their stock-market initial public offering (IPO), resulting in a USD 75 billion valuation – one of the 10 largest IPOs in the world, and the NYSE's biggest that year.

The company has had its highs, lows, and struggles since then, including massive layoffs and losses with COVID, but the stock price is only down 7.8 percent from its IPO price, which is more than many post-COVID companies can claim. Uber is one of the market's best performers.

Today, Uber has provided more than 10 billion rides and has more than 93 million active monthly users. It captured 71 percent of the market (and some say, created the market) for ride sharing. It operates in more than 900 cities worldwide and is one of the "gig economy's" biggest companies. The name has been "verbized" so that disrupted industries are said to have been "uberized." Start-ups often describe themselves as "Uber for . . . "

In just 12 years, they've grown from start-up underdog to uber-corporation. Early investors like Venture Capitalist Mark Suster, who famously ignored them, are kicking themselves.

Who would get into a car with a stranger? If there's a location-tracking system and a reputation-tracking system, apparently millions would.

In the age of the Internet, are any of us strangers, anymore?

Conclusions: How You, Too, Can Combine Unlikely Ideas to Create Radical Value

Figure 12.1: This book itself is a fusion – a sampler-quilt of companies, ideas, and people with insights you can apply in your own life.

> "Be yourself; everyone else is already taken."
> – Oscar Wilde

As I'm sure you've guessed by now, this book, itself, is a fusion of different ideas and innovations from different fields, but with insights that underlie them, tie them together, and should be useful to you in your journey.

It's also a sampler-quilt (see Figure 12.1). There's no way to include every high-value fusion in every industry. I've included ones my research assistants, Eswar Krishnan and Swesha Venkateshwaran, and I have come across. You surely know of others. I'd love to hear from you and have included my email address in my bio so you can share with me other examples you'd like me to share with others.

I've written and then re-read the above fusions, comparing them with one another and gleaning insights along the way. My insights and thoughts are below. Again, if you have others you'd like me to share, please contact me. Some of the greatest insights I shared in the original fusion book came from my interviewees, not me, which, again, is the point of fusion.

https://doi.org/10.1515/9783110703009-012

Integrating other people and ideas can take your creation to a whole new level.

Now, on to insights in a format I hope enhances their usefulness: situation ("let's assume"), recommendation ("now what"), and a reminder of the story (ies) that support and illustrate.

Open Out – Think Bigger, Feel More

Figure 12.2: Explore!

"Adventure is out there!"
– Ellie, *Up* (Pixar)

Let's assume: You want fresh ideas.

Now what: Explore broadly.

The first step in fusion is to open outward and explore broadly (see Figure 12.2). Here are some particular techniques you can try right now:

"Good artists copy. Great artists steal."
– Pablo Picasso
"If I have seen further, it is by standing on the shoulders of Giants."
– Isaac Newton

– *Don't invent – Explore analogies and copy (or "steal") from other industries, fields, nature, and so on.* Inventing and innovating are different. You don't have to invent something new in order to innovate, and, in fact, inventors use bits and pieces that were already invented in order to make something new. Inventors and innovators stand on the shoulders of giants. As we saw with the hospital emergency room that wanted to "get better," you have to get specific and define what you're looking for – what you're really trying to do. They decided "faster" and "right" were the essentials and sought an out-of-the-box example from a completely different situation. Once they went there and saw how things are done, they returned with so many great ideas they didn't have to invent. They had only to apply them. The key was to explore analogies and borrow. Key examples from above include:

- design thinking and the emergency room team that learned from a Formula 1 pit crew
- the children's magnetic resonance imaging (MRI); the troubled technician asked, "Why can't getting an MRI be like an amusement park or a children's museum?"
- the Rotterdam Eye Hospital, which looked to aviation for speed and quality improvements
- Minute Clinics and Commerce Bank, which both drew on the fast-food analogy – one for fast/affordable healthcare, and the other for fast/convenient financial services
- Ford and Oldsmobile, which crafted a new process for making cars, inspired by meat-packing
- biomimicry–since the natural world has already worked out many of our problems over millions of years, our analogies should include the wild (wilderness, that is, as well as "wild ideas")
- when Harvard Business School began, it had no teaching materials for its new field (corporate management), so it could not engage with students via lecture; by borrowing the case pedagogy from law and medicine, it not only solved the materials problem but also offered learning journeys that included personal transformation and practical skill-building
- Cirque du Soleil began with a dying industry (circus) and deeply thought through what people want; for fresh ideas, they looked to other industries that were giving people what they wanted, that is, ballet, cabaret, music concerts (including opera), street performance, and theatre. With deep thinking and broad ideas, they successfully "re-invented" the circus.
- *Use the crowd* – Nike lets people design their own, individual shoes, and large companies are increasingly embracing "open innovation" (collaborating with start-ups) and crowd-sourcing (for design ideas and more). Again, integrating other people and ideas can take your creation to a whole new level.
- *Try something no one else wants, and share shamelessly* – Dr. Ruth began her media career with a radio spot no one around her wanted. She gave it a try, and it was a remarkable success that then grew into a better time slot, longer timing, TV, print media, and beyond. She discussed openly and shared

publicly information that had been considered private – even taboo. Her original desire was to get contraceptive information out to the public, but with her openness to frank discussion, she discovered people needed information and advice on much more. Not only did the delivery media grow, but the topic grew, too, from an openness to try and openness to share.

– *Exercise empathy* – Design thinking (DT) begins with exploration of the problem to be solved and deeply engaging with people to understand their needs and desires. Design success begins with empathy. Although not known for empathy, lawyers also find they need to put their clients at ease in order to understand the problem and help effectively. Legal Grounds found a way to encourage ease and empathy by sharing conversation over coffee in comfortable surroundings.

Open In – Discover Deeper

Figure 12.3: Innovation isn't just about looking outward. You also have to look inward.

Looking outward isn't enough. Copying from somewhere else on a random basis doesn't usually work.

I know this sounds stupid, but people do it. A lot of people.

You have to think deeply about the problem you're trying to solve or the reason for radical creation of something new (see Figure 12.3). Go deep, then sideways, then up and out.

Cirque du Soleil didn't just borrow from other fields on a random basis. They were trying to re-think what a circus – and entertainment – really are. Depth and width lead to and reinforce (or discover) each other. You find one from the other, and you discover the other because you searched for the one:
- mystery and surprise – magic
- beauty – ballet
- fun – cabaret
- spontaneity and in-person energy – live theatre and street performance
- emotional awakening and catharsis – music concerts (including opera)

Let's assume: There's something under the surface of your "problem" or "opportunity."

Now what: Dig deeper.

- *Start with people's needs and desires* – Design thinking begins with people's needs and desires, and it's surprising how often people don't start with their customers/users. No one cares if you offer a shinier widget. They do care if you solve their problems and give them something they want better than how they fulfil their needs now. USD 1 billion start-up StockX, for example, began with "sneaker-heads" – people crazy about their sneaker collections. Allowing them to build their collections, trade, and manage their portfolios gave them joy and tapped into a passion.
- *Tap into people's love of fantasy* – Disney and Pixar provide people with visual and auditory fantasy. Disneyland and *Pokémon Go* help them experience it in real life.
- *Go to the "root" of the matter* – Google's citation rankings differ from Yahoo!'s not in surface marketing but in the "root of the matter." Google's search engine is different, based on a different way of finding what people want. Competition isn't putting "lipstick on a pig" and selling it (in marketing-speak). It's based on solving people's problems better and finding a way to tell them that this is different.
- *See patterns and play with them* – As we see with the NetForm and TrustSphere stories, if you see a pattern, you might be the only one, and that's actually fine. They looked "under" social patterns, mathematically modeled them (with new mathematical methods from NetForm's founder, Dr. Karen Stephenson), and delved deeply into how to manage them for good. First, are you the only one seeing this? Second, how can you explain it and get others to join in?

"Am I the only one seeing this?"
– Fillmore, *Cars* (Pixar)

Let's assume: You're not feeling creative (or don't think you are).

Now what: Connect with something deeper (or higher).

- *Drop your keys* – When Salvador Dali wanted inspiration, he sat in a chair with a spoon (or keys) in his hand above a tin pie plate. He sat there long enough to fall asleep envisioning his problem, and when he did fall asleep, the spoon or keys would fall to the tin plate and noisily wake him. While in this sleeping–wakeful state, he tapped into both his conscious and subconscious mind to address whatever he wanted to address. You can, too.
- *Take a shower* – Any time you do something "mindless" like walking in the woods, lap-swimming, or showering you escape your conscious mind and tap into the unconscious. For some of us, that means escaping the logical and tapping into the creative. When the Hubble telescope needed mirrors to focus its images, the program manager not only gained insight while in the shower but mirrored the design of the shower-head itself, solving a USD 4.7 billion problem.
- *Pray and meditate (and more)* – Not only do creative people walk, swim, shower, and do other things that relax them and open them to their subconscious/intuitive/creative selves, but very many of them pray and meditate. Some feel it opens them up to something inner or deeper, and some feel it opens them up to a bigger/brighter source of wisdom and creativity – God. The innovators I've interviewed include Buddhist, Christian, Jewish, Muslim, Hindu, Shaman, and more, and those who pursue a faith-based life also pursue faith-based creativity.

Let's assume: You're not happy with what you're doing or want to find something you love.

Now what: Explore yourself.

Not only does the answer lie deeper within the problem, but the creativity usually lies deeper within yourself. If you just do what you're told seeking outward success, you'll probably never tap into your own well of creativity. If you do look deeper within yourself, you may find creative answers designed into yourself, waiting to be unlocked when you land in a new problem.

- *Learn what you want, not what others tell you* – Charles Darwin refused to study medicine and theology (or just couldn't work up the energy to do it), in order to follow his own passions: natural history, biology, and geology. Once he followed his own passions, he integrated them in a way no one else did (perhaps as no one else could). Once his letters were published and gained popularity in the scientific community, his father eventually supported his life direction. Even if popularity and support don't come in your lifetime (think: van Gogh and Mendel), your unique combination and contribution may lay the foundation for something extremely significant beyond your lifetime. Would that make your life's work worthwhile?

– *Learn independently and do your own "thought experiments"* – Leonardo da Vinci couldn't go to school since he was the son of an unwed mother. So, he learned about the world broadly, powered by curiosity, under his own direction, and did "thought experiments." He integrated all he knew and discovered (since no one told him not to), unrestricted by the boundaries of formal fields or formal training. His disadvantage was an advantage. Do you have a disadvantage you could use to advantage? Even if you don't envision that you could use it to advantage, can you use it, anyway?

– *Be curious, "drop in," and journey* – Steve Jobs famously "dropped in" on a calligraphy class in college and pursued Zen Buddhism travels in India well before his success as a computer innovator. What do you love that has laid a foundation in your mind? Could your practical work afterwards draw on it in inspiring ways?

– *Travel* – Like Steve Jobs, Martin Rothblatt left college to travel internationally, during which time Martin envisioned uniting the world with satellite communication. Dropping out of college to take classes of interest (like Steve) or to explore (like Martin) are, for some people, the most productive times of their lives – a time to collect experiences, ideas, people, and connect them in powerful ways.

Collect Ideas, People, and More

Figure 12.4: Collect ideas, skills, people, and more before you need them – just because you like them. Then when you have a problem, do a focused search.

Like Steve Jobs and Martin Rothblatt, exploring outward can help you discover inward, and it can be a useful time to build a collection of people, ideas, skills, and more (see above sections on "Apple: The Art of Technology" and "Satellite Radio, United Therapeutics, and One of the World's Highest-Paid CEO's"). The collection isn't driven by particular problems you need to solve right now, but rather by your internal design, curiosity, and what interests you (see Figure 12.4).

Let's assume: You're bored by what you do or where you are.

Now what: Explore and collect.

- *Collect as you go* – What would you learn and do if you were a millionaire? Where would you go? What you learn and the resources you collect along the way are the materials with which you create value that supports the journey you've already started. In other words, instead of working and saving so you can live later, if you live now, you create more for living later than you would if you delayed being happy and being yourself. In even shorter words, money can't necessarily buy happiness, but happiness can often buy (or create) money (Abey and Ford, 2009; Meadows, 2020a). Start with learning, connecting, growth, and happiness. Don't plan to start without it and finish (magically) with it.
- *Grow up in diversity (no, you're never too old!)* – Paul Klee, Johannes Gutenberg, Gregor Mendel, and many, many more high-value lateral innovators grew up in diverse environments – nationally/culturally, religiously, workfields, and more. They began with a diverse mind-set and pursued their interests and work assuming it. If you haven't grown up with it, it's never too late to travel, live abroad, explore other fields, and pursue other initiatives to diversify your life and your mind. It's time to assume diverse is normal.

Let's assume: You think you're alone.

Now what: Connect.

- *Build your social network* – The people who drove the innovations in these pages grew social networks based on who interested them and then found that their connections either spurred new ideas or helped solve problems while developing these ideas (or both). In the agricultural age, it was important to have land, since agriculture was the source of wealth. Then, in the industrial age, it was important to build financial capital to build large enterprises. In the knowledge age, information capital was key to building new knowledge. Now, in this creative age, not only knowledge capital, but also social capital, is key. Both are grown through intensive collecting (build the capital) and also by employing the capital (use the capital) – collecting new people and ideas as you go. What social capital have you built? How do you use it and grow it?

– *Join a social network* – You don't have to build a social network from scratch. There are wonderful networks out there to join, such as NineSigma (P&G's consultants), which has a database of more than 2 million ideas and people/ institutions. The Indus Entrepreneurs (TiE) is a network of 15,000 entrepreneurs and funders worldwide who embrace new ideas and innovations to commercialize. Incubators and accelerators offer not only start-up services but also their networks of mentors, experts, and advisors. The world is full of networks and networks of networks to explore.

Although collecting starts here and is presented here, collecting doesn't finish before you sense a problem. Once you've found something to work on, spend some time searching and collecting in a focused manner. Do it broadly, with "outward openness" and analogous thinking. And do it deeply, exploring what people really want (like Cirque du Soleil) and by digging into history; exploring what didn't work but might be revived; as well as both your own and other people's collections. It's a key time to tap into both your and other people's social networks.

Sense the Problem/Opportunity . . . The Real One

Figure 12.5: Nothing can replace being there, feeling, asking, and listening for the real problem.

Let's assume: You think you know the problem.

Now what: Are you sure? Have you really "been there and done it?" Can you ask a better question (or lots more of them)?

- *Be there and live it* – A key feature of design thinking is to observe and engage with people where they live and work (see Figure 12.5). Don't just ask people what they need and want or even what they do. They often don't know. It's your job as an innovator to see them, ask why, and more. But you'll never do it sitting in your office, even if you invite them in for focus groups. Such groups and surveys are fine for well-defined problems, but radical and high-value innovation often happen where no one understands the problem . . . yet.
- *Ask why and what* – Cirque du Soleil deeply questioned what a circus is, what people want from entertainment, and why they seek the entertainment they do. The Tiger Center asked their forest service and community what they need and want. The answers they received were unexpected. Some of the answers you seek will come from "being there and living it" with your users. Some will come by asking why and what and discovering deeper.
- *Ask a better/deeper question* – In order to create a wrinkle-free fabric, Nine-Sigma helped P&G ask an effective, creative question to drive innovation – not, "How might we make fabric less wrinkly from the dryer?" but rather, "How might we relax surface tension of organic material?" Big answers don't usually come from little questions.
- *Ask, "How might we?"* – Questions are a key tool in design thinking (DT). We often use "stems" to drive our thinking, such as "How Might We." In fact, that is the classic DT question and contains three important concepts:
  - how – we assume we can do it; we just need to find how
  - might – teams delay "should" as long as possible in order to explore possibilities
  - we – it is essential to define early (and revise when necessary) who all the stakeholders are, in order to gain acceptance of any solution and in order to tap into multiple people's ideas
- *See the system* – If the problem is integrated, the solution might have to be integrated, as well. The Tiger Center is a good example of this. Because tigers, environment, and people can live in conflict or help one another, and because they either fall-and-fail or survive-and-thrive together, programs to help them have to be integrated. Likewise, Ford adopted a highly efficient production method (the assembly line) and had to pay workers "high" wages to balance production and consumption. ("Otherwise, how can they buy my cars?")

- *Look for waste* – When you look at the whole system, pay attention to what is wasteful from a whole-system perspective. For space travel to become routine, Elon Musk knew that single-use USD 20-million rocket boosters was too huge an economic waste. He had to introduce sustainability to space and make reusable rocket boosters. Airbnb and Uber put homes and cars to use that would otherwise spend most of their time sitting empty. There's often a way to make something out of nothing if only you'll look.

Let's assume: Your back is against the wall and you have to try, even knowing nothing about it.

Now what: Just do it.

- *Do the project experts won't* – Martine Rothblatt founded United Therapeutics not from some grand vision of drug development, but to develop one drug to save her daughter's life. The pharmaceutical company that began a potentially life-saving drug shelved the project because they had other high-potential projects, and this one had problems. Martine licensed and developed the drug not for profit but to save someone she loved, despite the fact that she was a satellite engineer, not a medical researcher. However, she had the motivation to succeed and made it happen. Likewise, Dr. Ravi Kumar Banda, from the original fusion book (Meadows, 2020a), took on a project his colleagues said was scientifically impossible. He wasn't saving a particular life, but he knew his project could save millions of lives. He wanted to work on "something worth failing" and with his team made something that didn't fail, which could save 10 million lives a year and USD 1.2 billion in healthcare costs.
- *Question experts' assumptions and what is really a cause versus effect* – Not only do experts drop high-risk projects, but given their training, they may be predisposed to failure. When Raffi Rembrand researched autism diagnosis, he questioned something (speech-in-noise recognition) and asked if it might be the cause of autism instead of an effect (Meadows, 2020a). Because he was a chemical engineer and not an autism specialist, he questioned an assumption in a way experts didn't. That led him to ground-breaking research and a new way to diagnose autism spectrum disorder (ASD) from birth with a hearing test, far earlier than age five with existing behavioral tests. Early diagnosis opens a pathway to effective therapy for 2 million people a year.

Fuse – and Re-Fuse

Figure 12.6: Fusing can be as explosive as lighting a fuse, but it's not always that easy.

Fusion depends on the pre-conditions above and is encouraged by them, but the final step is not automatic or predictably easy (see Figure 12.6). The fusion stories in this book include terrific struggles and amazing persistence. Here are a few insights gained through those hard journeys, as well as the joy that ignited them.

Let's assume: You love two things.

Now what: Can you combine them?

– *Opposites attract* – For those of us who enjoy the stability and resources of big companies and the agility and creativity of start-ups, Eric Ries' book, *The Lean Startup* and the "agile" movement that followed made sense. They combined big and small, structured and unstructured, wacky and conservative, and stable and unstable, in order to get the best of both (and escape the worst of both). What other opposites do you love (and hate) that you could combine, to derive the best of both?

– *The stranger, the better* – Corporates and start-ups were thought to be different worlds that couldn't combine, but apparently, they can. The biggest opposites can produce the most value-creating mashups. In the artistic arena, one of Salvador Dali's most famous (and valuable) paintings, *Living Still Life* (*Nature Morte Vivante)* visualized Einstein's energy, mass, and relativity theories. One of his finest film collaborations was with an unlikely co-creator – Walt Disney.

Let's assume: You're stuck.

Now what: Turn 180 degrees and go the opposite way.

- *Smooth to rough* – Millions of dollars went into research to make nuclear submarines and other marine craft more energy-efficient by making the hulls smoother. Then one day, someone asked why the fastest "fish" in the ocean is rough. Researchers turned 180 degrees, investigated the fluodynamics of rough surfaces, and found they were, indeed, headed in exactly the wrong direction. "Sharkskin" marine surfaces and swimwear have surfaced as not only energy-saving for large vessels, but "unfairly" Olympic-winning when worn by swimmers.
- *Up to down* – Similarly, humankind for centuries has looked up to birds and bats for flight-design inspiration. However, instead of looking upwards to aerodynamics, we've more recently looked downward to fluodynamics. Manta-ray-inspired aircraft have achieved significant advances. Where will we look next?
- *Ugly to beautiful* – Radiators have long been an ugly device to hide. The science behind thermal radiation shows us that the more surface area a radiator has, the more effective it is. One designer drew inspiration from Rococo art, with its swirls and florets, to design a beautiful radiator. What else might you showcase as beautiful, even though today it is considered ugly?

Let's assume: You're stuck.

Now what: Can you use something that didn't work – but now might?

- *Revive the glass* – Corning worked on stronger windshield glass in the 1960s and then shelved the technology. When Steve Jobs wanted strong glass for the iPhone, researchers revived the windshield glass for a new use, which created some of iPhone's "magic" and then kindled a new capability (wireless charging).
- *Combine it with the new vacuum* – The lightbulb was actually invented 77 years before Edison's commercially viable lightbulb. He used a newer, more powerful vacuum on old and new designs to craft his iconic invention, as well as a more effective incandescent material and high resistance that made central power distribution economically viable. If Thomas Edison wasn't afraid to re-use what "didn't work," should you be?
- *Apply the little-used drug to a new diagnosis* – Ritalin was a fast-acting blood pressure medicine and stimulant from 1944 that failed to become a best-seller. Only after new social trends (acceptance of psychoactive drugs and therapy) and a new diagnosis (ADHD in children) did it become a best-seller.

- *Basically, actively search your/someone's collection/history* – Look to your own or someone else's collection. Collecting is an important stage in Fusion because you can revive what didn't work but might work now. In some sense, you're doing it (collecting) by reading this book.

Let's assume: You see the integration, but no one else does.

Now what: Prove it.

- *Do the math* – Einstein saw the connection between energy and mass, and space and time. The concept was a breakthrough, but it was only accepted because he worked out the math, giving us his most famous equation ($E = mc^2$) and theory (relativity).
- *Invent the math* – Some of the math Einstein worked out was new – invented. Likewise, before Dr. Karen Stephenson founded NetForm, she had to create some of the mathematics she would use to model social systems. Combining her new mathematical techniques with other fields (anthropology, ethnography, computer programming, and management consulting) paved the way for her epiphany (seeing social patterns) to become an accepted methodology (social network modeling).

Let's assume: You have a great idea, and no one pays attention.

Now what: Make a multi-billion-dollar company like Airbnb, FedEx, and Uber.

- *Turn your school paper into a business* – FedEx was originally a class assignment (not highly marked), and Vaxess Technologies (award-winning company from the original fusion book) was a business plan for "Commercialization of Science" class. School is a great opportunity not only to collect new ideas, skills, and people, but also to take time to make a business plan for something that could become radical and big.
- *Ignore the "No's" until you get to "Yes"* – Airbnb and Uber were both ignored by venture capitalists. After all, everyone's mother has spent a lifetime telling us all not to enter a stranger's house or car. However, the Internet has made the world a small town again and enabled us to give social feedback when something is poorly done or dangerous. Something new has brought us back to an old way that works (hence the importance of "digging into" history). If they gave up after a "No" or a few "No's" or many "No's," would the ideas have died? Probably not. They would have been picked up by someone else who would have ignored every "No" until "Yes" and made those multi-billion-dollar companies.

Let's assume: You're scared to share your idea. (Someone might steal it!)

Now what: Calm down. Someone else probably thought of it already.

- *Their version is different* (almost undoubtedly) – Other online vacation rentals existed before Airbnb (for example, HomeAway, villa4vacation, Vrbo), but they were different (investment properties professionally managed, and so on). In fact, they still exist! There is room in most markets for multiple players. Just go ahead and make yours the best.
- *Join forces* – Sometimes, others working in the same space can help, since they've been pursuing it differently and have different capabilities. Litterati and Swedish plogging organizations aren't competing. They can help one another if one of them reaches out.

Let's assume: You still feel you should fiercely compete.

Now what: Consider "co-creating" or "competing by collaboration" even in a competitive context.

- *Have your user or supplier help and invest* – Apple and Corning collaborated to create gorilla glass, and Apple invested USD 200 million. It might be a good idea to collaborate with suppliers or customers.
- *Push control (and expenses) to someone else* – Supplier–retailer collaboration can also be hugely valuable to both. Walmart's tight partnership with suppliers for vendor-managed inventory means Walmart passes along cost (and control) to suppliers, and suppliers get more information and opportunities to sell. This collaboration is foundational to every strategy by the world's top retailer (Walmart).
- *Get (or be) a sidekick* – When Ralph Lauren was having growth pains (popularity without profitability), Ralph brought in a co-leader to run the business while Ralph focused on what he loved – design and marketing. The business flourished. I've seen this strategy before (yes, again, the original fusion book), with George Kolovos (creative force-of-nature) and MenuLog, which IPO'ed for USD 850 million.
- *Observe and experiment with real people* – The first and last phases of design thinking are to observe/engage and to prototype/experiment. Design thinkers don't design in a vacuum. Their innovations are accepted because they're grounded in reality and use a diverse set of people (designers, experts, and customers) from the start.
- *Piggyback on something already-successful* – When Zambian aid worker Simon Berry wanted to deliver life-saving anti-diarrheal kits to remote areas, he decided to piggy-back on Coca-Cola's already-successful distribution network.

- *Talk to your wife (or someone else's)* – Unfortunately, it would be a "hard sell" to get Coca-Cola to remove some of their products from the delivery crates, thus increasing their cost of delivery. The problem was solved by the aid-founder's wife. She looked at the crates and asked why they didn't just use the triangular space between the bottle necks. Of course! The kits were packaged into triangular delivery packs, and they got a free ride in Coca-Cola crates, which are distributed to 200 countries around the world. Is this just a creative fluke? Apparently, no. Walt Disney's wife, for example, didn't like the sound of the original character name, "Mortimer Mouse." He was re-named "Mickey," and the rest is history.

> "I am your WIFE! I am the greatest good you're EVER gonna get!"
> – Mrs. Frozone, *The Incredibles*

Let's assume: Someone does steal your idea, and now competitors and copycats are coming out of the wood-work.

Now what: Get them to fight one another.

- When Atari founder Nolan Bushnell introduced the world's first personal arcade games and TTL (transistor-to-transistor logic), patents took three years to process. In the meantime, a gaggle of copycats arose, and Magnavox declared Atari a copycat. In a brilliant move, Bushnell settled with Magnavox and stipulated in the settlement that Magnavox would be in charge of disciplining other copycats. This freed Atari to pursue new developments and continue as a growing business without draining its resources to fight a gaggle that could only be fought with a big player like Magnavox. Do you have opponents you might incite to fight one another instead of you?

Let's assume: You started one thing and others are evolving it.

Now what: Roll with it.

- *Enjoy your piece of the pie, even if you made a big pie and took a small piece* – Atari grew (USD 143 million), but the gaming industry grew much, much bigger (USD 162 billion). Is it a failure story? Not necessarily. Atari still grew and benefited from their creation. Sometimes others will grow more. You don't have to own the whole pie as long as you get a good slice.
- *Do the weddings* – A Little White Chapel's drive-through weddings were created for couples with disabilities. However, couples without disabilities loved the idea and came in droves. Fine. In solving one problem, you may solve others or solve no problem at all. As long as you've created something people enjoy, I guess there isn't a problem, which is good.

- *Watch the legacy grow* – Your fusion may be popularized years later by someone else (or you could be that someone else!), as we see with:
  - World Wide Web (multiple research networks developed over years)
  - GPS (government satellite network then commercialized)
  - Aerobics (conceptualized by doctors then popularized by celebrities)
  - Ritalin (developed by a drug designer then popularized decades later)
  - Coca-Cola (founded by a morphine addict who imported coca-wine from France, built over 129 years into a global powerhouse)

Let's assume: You fail.

Now what: Should you drop it or try again?

- *Launch it a second time* – Surprisingly, going bankrupt doesn't mean you've got a bad idea or even that it's the wrong time to launch. Henry J. Heinz saw two big trends coming together in a new way – urbanization and new canning technology – and believed people would start to buy pre-packaged foods instead of harvesting and canning food themselves. The first Heinz company launched successfully but went bankrupt from cashflow and operations problems. So it failed, and it's time to do something else, right? Wrong. He learned his business-management lessons, knew the trends were just as powerful as they were before (if not more so), and started the company again. The Kraft Heinz Co. is now worth USD 50 billion.
- *Launch it a third time* – Airbnb launched three times before they found a venture capitalist that saw potential in their idea and invited them into Y Combinator. Apparently, three times isn't necessarily a "strike out." It could be the winning strike.
- *Launch a new thing* – Walt Disney's Laugh-O-Gram Studio went bankrupt, and he went to Hollywood with USD 40 in his pocket to join his brother, Roy, and build something new. That new thing grew into The Walt Disney Company.
- *Get up at 4:00 am, again* – For years, Scott Adams (creator of the Dilbert cartoon series) awoke every workday at 4:00 am to draw cartoons before going to work at the phone company. He drew new characters, developed new stories and insights, honed his craft, and drew on his corporate experience to create something people wanted to see and would relate to. He sold a few cartoons, grew his practice, and finally developed it into a full-time job – the job he wanted instead of the phone company. Was every day a failure because it wasn't a day as a full-time cartoonist? Or was every day a success, because he took another step forward toward that career? In some regard, it doesn't matter. It only mattered that he did it – every day.

Figure 12.7: Now might not be the time, but that doesn't mean the idea is dead.

Let's assume: What you want to do isn't possible right now.

Now what: Bide your time but keep scanning.

- *About 40 percent of start-up success is timing* – Idealab founder Bill Gross named his firm for what he thought was the most important element of start-up success – a great idea. However, when he studied more than 200 new ventures to find the key elements of success, he was stunned. The #1 element that accounted for more than 40 percent of success was timing (see Figure 12.7). Uber knew they could get customers, but they didn't know where they'd get their drivers. Luckily for them, the US economy experienced a recession just before they launched, and newly laid off workers became drivers.
- *Strike when most of the pieces are ready* – For Nolan Bushnell at Atari, the mainframe age was too soon for mass-market computer games. Because the machines were so expensive, only people who were working on mainframes could create and play games. So, he waited. Minicomputers were also too expensive. However, with the advent of minis, he decided it was time to simplify a game, and when he and fellow-engineer Ted Dabney developed transistor-to-transistor logic, they were able to create a single-use device. Personal gaming was born.
- *The lightbulb was invented 77 years before Edison's lightbulb* – Humphry Davy invented the first electric light in 1802, followed by 20 more inventors

seeking to commercialize it. When Thomas Edison came along in 1879, his version outperformed the others because he had a better vacuum, effective incandescent material, and achieved high resistance, making centralized power distribution commercially viable. Similar to Idealab's new ventures, the ideas need to be good, but the timing is also essential. Have recent advances made this the right time to pursue a problem you've put on hold?

Let's assume: You succeed.

Now what: Where else can you take it?

- *You've solved your own problem, so offer it to others* – The founders of Airbnb were trying to afford their rent. The founder of Coca-Cola was trying to fight his morphine addiction. Good problem solvers solve their problems. *Entrepreneurs solve other people's problems.*
- *Use your hammer on a screw* – Sometimes, when I'm fixing something with a self-driving screw, bystanders are surprised to see me first use a hammer on my screw. It makes sense, though. First drive the pointy end into the wood with a hammer, then screw it in with a screwdriver. That analogy works for other things, too. One tool can be used very effectively in another place, where you don't think it belongs. NVIDIA, for example, achieved success in gaming with their simulation engine. They grew into the NVIDIA they are today by taking their solution to other problems, such as medical research. Drug development looks like a very different problem in a very different industry, but at depth it's not. The gaming simulation hammer has helped many medical researchers drive their developments forward.
- *Assume you're a hammer – go hammer a screw* – Bill Gates was very good with technology (yes, I know how dumb that sounds), and he was passionate about eradicating polio. By applying high-tech tracking and mapping of polio outbreaks in Africa, he and his team discovered they were occurring at jurisdictional borders where different groups of vaccine distributors thought someone else was covering the area. They revised their distribution methods, and now two out of three wild polio virus strains have been completely eradicated. More than 95 percent of Africa's population has been vaccinated, and Africa has been declared polio-free from the last remaining wild strain of the virus (Scherbel-Ball, 2020). All continents but Asia have been declared free of wild poliovirus, and only Afghanistan and Pakistan remain wild-polio-endemic.
- *Have a "Think Week"* – One of the things Bill Gates does each year in order to apply himself to new problems is to take a broad variety of books to his beach house and have a "think week," in which he explores, contemplates,

and connects problems and possible approaches to pursue. When was the last time you had a "think week"?

Let's assume: We succeeded but now face rejection.

Now what: Keep going.

Wasn't this supposed to be sweet success? . . .

- *Coca-Cola* began as commercialized coca-wine from Paris. Then Prohibition came along, and alcohol was banned (the small dose of cocaine was fine). So, they had to remove alcohol from their coca-wine. No matter. The company's reformulated "intellectual beverage and temperance drink" combined ingredients from the coca plant and cola (or kola) nut and continued to grow in popularity.
- *Sharkskin swimwear* was banned at the Olympics after 96 percent of medals were awarded to sharkskin-swimwearing swimmers. However, it is still a commercial product, and the attention gained during its one and only Olympic event surely couldn't have been bad publicity.
- *Airbnb and Uber* faced enormous struggles after their initial success. No matter. All part of growth. Airbnb faced marketing problems early on because of poor photography and presentation. They investigated in-person, offered free photography and marketing services, and grew. Now hosts can see sites that sell well and copy the marketing style. Some cities banned Airbnb, but they grow, nonetheless. Uber faced protests from licensed taxi drivers, as well as city ordinance restrictions, but they grow, nonetheless. You'll face fights and struggles after your initial success, so expect it, and expect a problem-solving innovation journey during growth and scaling.
- *Walt Disney* wanted to create Disneyland but found it an uphill battle to obtain funding, location, and support. It caused a rift between him and his brother, Roy, that never healed. Walt borrowed money against his life insurance policy to buy an orange grove and start the Disneyland project. Even with the success of achieving an opening day, the first two weeks saw forged entry tickets, a plumbing strike (so no water fountains in hot California), unfriendly security personnel, long lines, sprinkler malfunction, gas leak, near-capsize of a Mark Twain boat, and grumpy customers wasting time paying for individual rides. Every difficulty was solved – one by one. Success leads to problems, which leads to solutions, which cycles again. Success means growing comfortable – and internally rewarded and energized – in the midst of that cycle.

Let's assume: You succeed.

Now what: Can you do it again?

Many of the leaders and enterprises in this book fused, then fused again. Fusion doesn't seem to be a one-off event. It seems to be a cycling journey.

- *Amazon* began with books and Internet, then folded in other products (making it a marketplace, not a bookstore), then cloud and other services (commercializing what they had developed internally and were innovating for themselves).
- *Disney* began with "still art" combined into sequential animation; then integrated animation and live action; then integrated animation and sound; further fused greyscale cinema and technicolor; moved on to music and video; then integrated video, consumer products, and theme parks; leading to integration of large and small organizations (Disney and Pixar).
- *Elon Musk* began with software, moved on to cars, and continued to space travel.
- *Martine Rothblatt* launched satellite radio, moved on to healthcare, and is now pursuing artificial intelligence, theology, and human-technology integration via mind cloning for virtual immortality.
- *Netflix* offered videos via postal service, then re-invented itself into streaming.
- *Fusion* began as a multimedia article collection, became a book, and is now a book series. I don't place myself in the same league as the above businesses and founders, but does it matter? What can you begin and build?

> "Thanks for the adventure. Now go have a new one!"
> – Ellie, *Up* (Pixar)

Figure 12.8: You've helped me learn, and I hope you've learned – now use the ideas for a new adventure!

Thank you. That pretty well sums up what's happened. Innovators have made our lives better. They've stood on one another's shoulders. In writing this book, I've learned from them in order to share with you. Thank you all.

I hope you've learned from them, too, and that my small insights are useful. Now it's time to use them and have a new adventure of your own (see Figure 12.8). I offer you every blessing for your journey.

Can I include you in my next book?

Bibliography

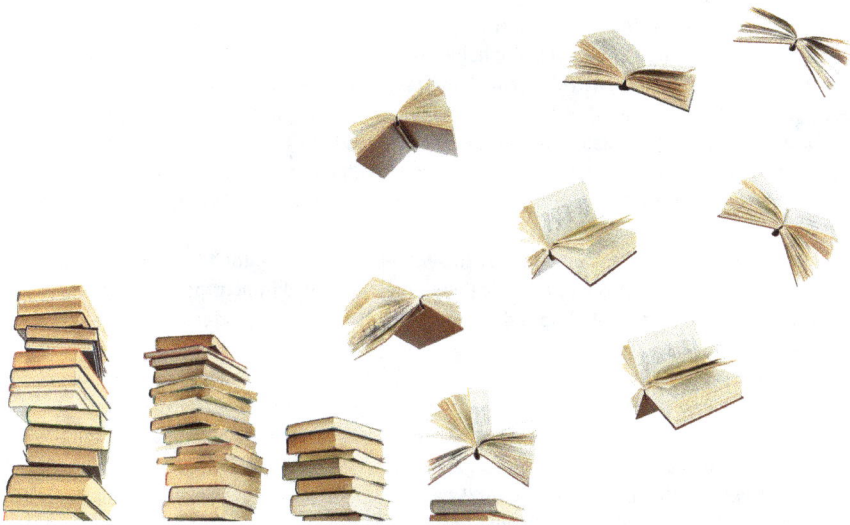

Figure 13.1: Better grab a reference before they all fly away . . .

Abey, Arun, and Ford, Andrew. (2009). *How Much is Enough? Making Financial Decisions that Create Wealth and Wellbeing*. Austin, TX: Greenleaf Book Group.

Adams, Scott. (1996). *The Dilbert Principle: A Cubicle Eye's View of Bosses, Meetings, Management Fads and Other Workplace Afflictions*. New York: Harper Business.

Allan, A. (2014). *Business Model Innovation: Concepts, Analysis, and Cases* (2nd ed.). Abingdon, United Kingdom: Routledge.

Anand, U. (2021, February 4). What's the Value of a Tree? Age Multiplied by ₹74.5k: SC Panel. *Hindustan Times*. Retrieved from https://www.hindustantimes.com/india-news/whats-the-value-of-a-tree-age-multiplied-by-74-5k-sc-panel-101612377235565.html

Apurva, P. (2019, March 9). This Mumbai-based Startup Helps Get You in Shape and Earns You Goodies as Well [blog post]. Retrieved from https://yourstory.com/2019/03/mumbai-fitness-startup-stepsetgo-tb06o3355b

Art Link International. (n.d.). Kneel, P. [blog post]. Retrieved from https://www.artlinkinternational.com/artists/paul-klee/

Assembly Line. (n.d.). In Wikipedia. Retrieved from https://en.wikipedia.org/wiki/Assembly_line

ATAG.org. (2020, September). Facts and Figures. Retrieved from https://www.atag.org/facts-figures.html

Bagla, Pallava. (2017, July 16). Making the Hidden Visible: Economic Valuation of Tiger Reserves In India. *Hindustan Times*. Retrieved from https://www.hindustantimes.com/environment/saving-2-tigers-gives-more-value-than-the-cost-of-mangalyaan/story-s17glKMyLKHeuEHzwpidZM.html and (reprint) https://davidshepherd.org/news/green-accounting-highlights-value-of-wild-tigers/

https://doi.org/10.1515/9783110703009-013

Bajari, Tim. (2017, September 11). How Corning's Crash Project for Steve Jobs Helped Define the iPhone [blog post]. Retrieved from https://www.fastcompany.com/40493737/how-cornings-crash-project-for-steve-jobs-helped-define-the-iphone

Baum, L. Frank. (1900). *The Wonderful Wizard of Oz*. Chicago: George M. Hill Company.

BBC News. (2019, March 26). How a Kingfisher Helped Reshape Japan's Bullet Train [video]. Retrieved from https://www.bbc.com/news/av/science-environment-47673287

Bellis, Mary. (2019, March 21). History of the Fax Machine [blog post]. Retrieved from https://www.thoughtco.com/history-of-the-fax-machine-1991379

Berliet, Melanie. (2009, July 22). "Twelve Women Who Changed the Way We Look at Sex." *Vanity Fair*. Retrieved from https://www.vanityfair.com/news/2009/07/sexuality-timeline.

Bhamra, T. (2019, March 7). Trevor Baylis: The Wind-Up Radio Inventor Who Forced Companies to Take Sustainable Design Seriously [blog post]. Retrieved from https://theconversation.com/trevor-baylis-the-wind-up-radio-inventor-who-forced-companies-to-take-sustainable-design-seriously-92967

Birla, M. (2005, July 15). *FedEx Delivers: How the World's Leading Shipping Company Keeps Innovating and Outperforming the Competition*. Hoboken, NJ: Wiley. Retrieved from https://books.google.com.sg/books?id=b7qKi-CzlEsCandpg=PT23andlpg=PT23anddq=fedex+combined+unrelated+ideas+togetherandsource=blandots=yrLU2Elxorandsig=ACfU3U3vw2a0MVNuZqhNSRu9OcPUgofY5wandhl=enandsa=Xandved=2ahUKEwiOvrj-pr7mAhWd7HMBHXalDzIQ6AEwAnoECAoQAQ#v=onepageandqandf=false

Brown, Tim. (n.d.) Design Thinking Defined. Retrieved from https://designthinking.ideo.com/

(2014, March 17). Elephant Trunk-Influenced Bionic Handling Assistant by Festo Learns like a Baby [blog post]. Retrieved from https://www.designboom.com/technology/elephant-trunk-influenced-bionic-handling-assistant-by-festo-learns-like-a-baby-03-17-2014/

Bulbs.com Learning Center. (n.d.) History of the Lightbulb [blog post]. Retrieved from https://www.bulbs.com/learning/history.aspx

CBC. (2019, May 3). Stitching up Surgical Cuts with Slug Slime [blog post]. Retrieved from https://www.cbc.ca/radio/quirks/may-4-2019-brain-resuscitation-hippos-supply-algae-skeletons-slug-surgical-glue-and-more-1.5119885/stitching-up-surgical-cuts-with-slug-slime-1.5119907

Cheer Bell Gallery. (2016, March 24). Salvador Dali's 7 Most Expensive Paintings [blog]. Retrieved from https://www.cheerbell.com/en/blog/salvador-dalis-7-most-expensive-paintings#:~:text=A%20staggering%20%2422.4%20million

Cooper, Hewitt. (2018, January 12). Reinventing Functionality [blog post]. Retrieved from https://www.cooperhewitt.org/2018/01/12/reinventing-functionality/

Cooper, Kenneth. (1968). *Aerobics*. Lanham, MD: M. Evans and Company (now part of Rowman & Littlefield).

Crosby, Tim. (2008, 10 April). History of the Fax Machine [blog post]. Retrieved from https://electronics.howstuffworks.com/gadgets/fax/history-of-fax2.htm

Cruikshank, J. (1987). *Delicate Experiment: The Harvard Business School 1908-1945*. Boston, MA: Harvard Business Review Press.

Dance, Jeff. (2017, August 10). Innovation Principle #7: Seek Inspiration [blog post]. Retrieved from https://www.freshconsulting.com/innovation-principle-7-seek-inspiration/

Danziger, Pam. (2017, April 24). Two Worlds Collide at Ralph Lauren – Mass and "Class" [blog post]. Retrieved from https://unitymarketingonline.com/two-worlds-collide-at-ralph-lauren-mass-class/

Economist, The. (2018, August 25). Air-Conditioners Do Good, But At A High Environmental Cost. *The Economist.* Retrieved from https://www.economist.com/international/2018/08/25/air-conditioners-do-great-good-but-at-a-high-environmental-cost

Elon Musk. (n.d.). In Wikipedia. Retrieved September 8, 2020 from https://en.wikipedia.org/wiki/Elon_Musk

Emilie. (2011, April 28). The Fine Art of Bringing Together Unrelated Ideas [blog post]. Retrieved from https://puttylike.com/the-fine-art-of-bringing-together-unrelated-ideas/

Fischer, R. (2004). The Creation of Disneyland [blog post]. Retrieved from http://www.plosin.com/beatbegins/projects/fischer.html

Fisk, Peter. (2015). *Gamechangers: Creating Innovative Strategies for Business and Brands: New Approaches to Strategy, Innovation and Marketing.* Chichester, UK: John Wiley and Sons, Ltd.

Frisk, P. (2011). *Creative Genius: An Innovation Guide for Business Leaders, Border Crossers and Game Changers.* Mankato, MN: Capstone.

Gladwell, M. (2002). *The Tipping Point: How Little Things Can Make a Big Difference.* Boston, MA: Little Brown and Co. (Hachette).

Glaz, R. and Muscolino, H. (2017, June). Fax Market Pulse: Trends, Growth and Opportunities. IDC [white paper]. Retrieved from https://www.opentext.com/file_source/OpenText/en_US/PDF/opentext-idc-survey-fax-market-pulse%20-en.pdf.

Grand View Research. (2017, July). *Scratch Resistant Glass Market Size Worth $8.17 Billion By 2025* [research report]. Retrieved from https://www.grandviewresearch.com/press-release/global-scratch-resistant-glass-market

Grand View Research. (2019, September). *Medical Adhesives Market Size, Share and Trends Analysis Report.* Retrieved from https://www.grandviewresearch.com/industry-analysis/medical-adhesives-market

Groysberg, B., and Connolly Baden, K. (2018). TrustSphere: Building a Market for Relationship Analytics [case]. Boston, MA: Harvard Business School [9-418-070].

Harvard School of Public Health. (2020). The Most Expensive Healthcare System in the World [blog post]. Retrieved November 9, 2020 from https://www.hsph.harvard.edu/news/hsph-in-the-news/the-most-expensive-health-care-system-in-the-world/

Harvard University. (2017, July 27). Sticky When Wet: Strong Adhesive for Wound Healing [blog post]. Retrieved from https://phys.org/news/2017-07-sticky-strong-adhesive-wound.html

Hunter Marnie. (2010, October 4). Happy Anniversary, Wheeled Luggage! [blog post]. Retrieved from http://edition.cnn.com/2010/TRAVEL/10/04/wheeled.luggage.anniversary/index.html

IATA. (2020, November). Fuel Fact Sheet. Retrieved from https://www.iata.org/en/iata-repository/pressroom/fact-sheets/fact-sheet–fuel/

Ice Palace. (n.d.). In Wikipedia. Retrieved June 23, 2020 from https://en.m.wikipedia.org/wiki/Ice_palace

Industry Networkers. (2018, September 25). Sahara Forest Project: Greening the World's Deserts [blog post]. Retrieved from https://www.industry-networker.com/indy-4-18-greening-the-worlds-dese

Internet Association. (2019, September 26). The Internet Sector Created 6 Million Jobs, $2.1 Trillion in GDP in 2018, New IA Research Finds [press release]. Retrieved from https://internetassociation.org/news/the-internet-sector-created-6-million-jobs-2-1-trillion-in-gdp-in-2018-new-ia-research-finds/

Jaga. (n.d.). Stylish Designer Radiator – Heatwave [blog post]. Retrieved from http://www. jaga.co.uk/designer-radiators/heatwave/

Jaruzelski, B., Staack, V., and Goehle, B. (2014, winter). Proven Paths to Innovation Success: Ten Years of Research Reveal the Best R&D Strategies for the Decade Ahead. *Strategy +Business*.

Jorislaarmanlab. (n.d.). Heatwave 2003 [blog post]. Retrieved from https://www.jorislaarman. com/work/heatwave/

Kannadasan, A. (2015, January 9). Dhoti Cool [blog post]. Retrieved from https://www.the hindu.com/features/metroplus/dhoti-cool/article6772071.ece

Kestenbaum, R. (2018, September 9). The Biggest Trends in the Beauty Industry [blog post]. Retrieved from https://www.forbes.com/sites/richardkestenbaum/2018/09/09/beauty-in dustry-biggest-trends-skin-care-loreal-shiseido-lauder/#44bdca756982

Kirsch, M. (2011, September 18). Minute Clinics: The McDonalds Version of Healthcare? [blog post]. Retrieved from https://medcitynews.com/2011/09/minute-clinics-the-mcdonalds- version-of-healthcare/

Klein, J. (2019, March 26). What Termites Can Teach us about Cooling our Buildings [blog post]. Retrieved from https://www.nytimes.com/2019/03/26/science/termite-nest- ventilation.html

Kovaleski, Dave. (2020, February 25). If You Invested $500 in Uber's IPO, This Is How Much Money You'd Have Now. *The Motley Fool*. Retrieved from https://www.fool.com/investing/ 2020/02/25/if-you-invested-500-in-ubers-ipo-this-is-how-much.aspx#:~:text=Ultimately %2C%20Uber%20announced%20an%20IPO,Stock%20Exchange%20on%20May%2010

Larson, A. (2020, August 25). See How This Cat Café Sustains the Perfect Feline Community. *All Creatures* (Guideposts publication). Retrieved May 3, 2021 from https://www.guideposts. org/friends-and-family/pets/cats/see-how-this-cat-cafe-sustains-the-perfect-feline- community

Lego Serious Play. (n.d.). In Wikipedia. Retrieved June 23, 2020 from https://en.wikipedia. org/wiki/Lego_Serious_Play

Lehrer, Jonah. (2011, October 7). Steve Jobs: "Technology Alone Is Not Enough." *The New Yorker*. Retrieved from https://www.newyorker.com/news/news-desk/steve-jobs-technol ogy-alone-is-not-enough

Losey, K. (2019, September 10). The Future of Innovation is Here: 8 Inventions from Nature's Laboratory [blog post]. Retrieved from https://biomimicry.org/the-future-of-innovation-is- here-8-inventions-from-natures-laboratory/

Magazine review – *Computers & Graphics*. (2001). ARQuake [blog post]. Retrieved from https://ultimatehistoryvideogames.jimdofree.com/arquake/

Mahapatra, C. (2019, August 3). Conserving Tigers Has Economic Benefits, Too. BloombergQuint. Retrieved from https://www.bloombergquint.com/economy-finance/con serving-tigers-has-economic-benefits-too#:~:text=IIFM%20suggests%20that%20there% 20are,gene%2Dpool%20of%20innumerable%20organisms

MarketResearch.com. (2016). Online Fax Market – Global Outlook and Forecast 2017–2022 [research report]. Retrieved from https://www.marketresearch.com/Arizton-v4150/Online- Fax-Global-Outlook-Forecast-11296755/

Matusow, J. (2010, January 25). 2009 Company of the Year L'Oréal: Believable Beauty [blog post]. Retrieved from https://www.beautypackaging.com/issues/2010-01/view_features/ 2009-company-of-the-year-loreal-believable-be/

Mccauley, L. (2000, June 30). Legal Grounds [blog post]. Retrieved from https://www.fastcom pany.com/39902/legal-grounds

McTigue, Kathleen. (2019, October 2). *Economic Benefits of the Global Positioning System to the U.S. Private Sector Study*. National Institute of Standards and Technology (Technology Partnerships Office) [research report]. Retrieved from https://www.nist.gov/news-events/ news/2019/10/economic-benefits-global-positioning-system-us-private-sector-study#:~: text=For%20the%20United%20States%20alone,day%20impact%20to%20the%20nation

Meadows, C. (2020a). *Innovation through Fusion: Combining Innovative Ideas to Create High-Impact Solutions*. Berlin: De Gruyter.

Meadows, C. (2020b). *Innovation through Fusion: High-Impact Innovation Method, Stories, and Community*. Singapore: Gnowbe.

Meadows, C. (2020c). *Innovation through Fusion: High-Value Lateral Innovation Intro*. Singapore: Gnowbe.

Medgaget. (2021, February 16). Genetic Testing Market Size [Market Research Release]. Retrieved from https://www.medgadget.com/2021/02/genetic-testing-market-size-is-pro jected-to-reach-usd-22834-19-million-by-2024-at-a-cagr-of-11-50-global-industry-trends-share-growth-analysis-top-companies-revenue.html#:~:text=Categories-,Genetic%20Test ing%20Market%20Size%20Is%20Projected%20To%20Reach%20USD%2022%2C834.19, Growth%20Analysis%2C%20Top%20Companies%20Revenue

Michalko, M. (2012, February 19). Allow Your Ideas to Have Sex with Other Ideas to Create New Ideas [blog post]. Retrieved from https://www.creativitypost.com/article/allow_your_ ideas_to_have_sex_with_other_ideas_to_create_new_ideas

Michalko, M. (2012, July 17). Salvador Dali's Creative Thinking Technique [blog post]. Retrieved from https://www.creativitypost.com/article/salvador_dalis_creative_thinking_technique

Miko, I. (2008). Gregor Mendel and the Principles of Inheritance. *Nature Education* 1(1): 134.

Ministry of Environment, Forest and Climate Change, Government of India. (2016, April 12). 3rd Asia Ministerial Conference on Tiger Conservation Conference Proceedings.

Morton, M.C. (2008, August 28). A Whale of a Wind Turbine [blog post]. Retrieved from https://www.earthmagazine.org/article/whale-wind-turbine

Nerdfitness. (n.d.). What is Nerd Fitness? [blog post]. Retrieved from https://www.nerdfitness. com/about-2/#what_is_nerd_fitness

NIH. (2017, August 8). Medical Glue Inspired by Sticky Slug Mucus [blog post]. Retrieved from https://www.nih.gov/news-events/nih-research-matters/medical-glue-inspired-sticky-slug-mucus

Nikolaus, F., Marion, P., and Martin, S. (2014, November 21). Sometimes the Best Ideas Come from Outside Your Industry [blog post]. Retrieved from https://hbr.org/2014/11/some times-the-best-ideas-come-from-outside-your-industry

OSV. (2017, March 7). A Brief History of the Smart Car: From the Swatchmobile to the Electric for Two [blog post]. Retrieved from https://www.osv.ltd.uk/history-of-the-smart-car/

Parsons, Elly. (2019, July 26). The Lilium Jet is Inspired by Gliding Manta Ray, New Sketches Reveal [blog post]. Retrieved from https://www.wallpaper.com/lifestyle/lilium-air-jet-new-sketches-revealed#pic_268052

Paul Klee. (n.d.). In Wikipedia. Retrieved June 23, 2020 from https://en.m.wikipedia.org/wiki/ Paul_Klee Piazza Geri

Pereira, Lorenzo. (2016, July 24). These are the Most Expensive Paul Klee Paintings Sold in the Auction Room. *Widewalls*. Retrieved from https://www.widewalls.ch/magazine/paul-klee-paintings

Reference for Business. (n.d.). In Reference for Business – Company History Index. Retrieved September 8, 2020 from https://www.referenceforbusiness.com/history2/44/Polo-Ralph-Lauren-Corporation.html

Ralph Lauren Corporation. (n.d.). In Wikipedia. Retrieved September 8, 2020 from https://en.wikipedia.org/wiki/Ralph_Lauren_Corporation#:~:text=Ralph%20Lauren%20started%20The%20Ralph,menswear%20%20%27Polo%27%20in%201968.

Refresher. (2008, February 9). Weird Combinations Work [blog post]. Retrieved from http://www.refresher.com/weird-combinations-work/

Revathy, L.N. (2015, February 14). Ramraj Launches "Velcro Pocket" Dhoti [blog post]. Retrieved from https://www.thehindubusinessline.com/companies/ramraj-launches-velcro-pocket-dhoti/article6896228.ece

Ries, Eric. (2011). *The Lean Startup: How Today's Entrepreneurs Use Continuous Innovation to Create Radically Successful Businesses*. Redfern, NWS, Australia: Currency Press.

Rizzy, Cailey. (2020, February 12). Airbus Unveils Design for Manta-Ray-Shaped Plane That Will Cut Carbon Emissions. *Travel+Leisure*. Retrieved from https://www.travelandleisure.com/travel-news/passenger-fined-assaulting-delta-flight-attendant-mask-rules

Rowe, Peter. (1987). *Design Thinking*. Cambridge, MA: MIT Press.

Saenz, A. (2010, September 27). Festo Turns Elephant's Trunk into Awesome Robot Arm [video]. Retrieved from https://singularityhub.com/2010/09/27/festo-turns-elephants-trunk-into-awesome-robot-arm-video/

Safehaven.com. (2018, February 9). New Tech Could Transform the $2 Trillion Auto Industry. FN Media Group and PRNewswire. Retrieved from https://www.prnewswire.com/news-releases/new-tech-could-transform-the-2-trillion-auto-industry-673561583.html

Samuel, A.N. (2017). The History of Time for Capsule Endoscopy. *Annals of Translational Medicine* 5(9): 194.

Sano, Hideyuki. (2016, July 19). Nintendo's Market Cap Doubles to $42 Billion Since Pokémon GO Launch. Reuters Technology News. Retrieved from https://www.reuters.com/article/us-nintendo-pokemon-stocks-idUSKCN0ZZ01Z

Sato, Courtney. (2013, June 25). How Design Thinking Can Make You a Better Leader [blog post]. Retrieved from https://www.constellationr.com/blog-news/how-design-thinking-can-make-you-better-leader

Scherbel-Ball, Naomi. (2020, August 25). Africa Declared Free of Wild Polio in "Milestone." BBC News. Retrieved from https://www.bbc.com/news/world-africa-53887947

Schroeder, Bernhard. (2019, September 23). What Is the Most Important Element of a Successful Startup? Forbes. Retrieved from https://www.forbes.com/sites/bernhardschroeder/2019/09/23/what-is-the-most-important-element-of-a-successful-startup-hint-its-not-the-idea-team-business-model-or-funding-dollars/?sh=3e4a5925727c

Schuessler, Jennifer. (2012, June 21). "Audiences Can Now Analyze Dr. Ruth." The New York Times. Retrieved from https://www.nytimes.com/2012/06/24/theater/new-play-about-dr-ruth-westheimer.html.

Science.jrank. (n.d.). Assembly Line [blog post]. Retrieved from https://science.jrank.org/pages/558/Assembly-Line-History.html

Sharkey, J. (2010, October 4). Reinventing the Suitcase by Adding the Wheel [blog post]. Retrieved from https://www.nytimes.com/2010/10/05/business/05road.html?mtrref=undefinedandassetType=REGIWALLandmtrref=www.nytimes.comandgwh=3E550FFA21F53523CAD650F39C99E245andgwt=payandassetType=REGIWALL

Sheppard, B., Sarrazin, H., Kouyoumjian, G., and Dore, F. (2018, October 25). Business Value by Design. McKinsey Quarterly.

Silvestre, D. (2018, September 7). Steve Jobs Insane Productivity Secrets [blog post]. Retrieved from https://medium.com/swlh/steve-jobs-insane-productivity-secrets-470e99c482f6

Simmons, M. (2018, April 6). People Who Have "Too Many Interests" Are More Likely to Be Successful According to Research [blog post]. Retrieved from https://medium.com/accelerated-intelligence/modern-polymath-81f882ce52d

Sloane, P. (2003, September 26). How Unusual Combinations Lead to Breakthrough Ideas [blog post]. Retrieved from https://innovationmanagement.se/imtool-articles/how-unusual-combinations-lead-to-breakthrough-ideas/

Sloane, P. (2007). *The Innovative Leader: How to Inspire Your Team and Drive Creativity.* London: Kogan Page.

Smith, Adam. (1776, March 9). *An Inquiry into the Nature and Causes of the Wealth of Nations.* London: W. Strahan and T. Cadell.

Smolan, Rick and Erwitt, Jennifer. (2012). *The Human Face of Big Data.* New York: Against All Odds Productions.

Sorensen, Charles E. (2006). *My Forty Years with Ford.* Detroit, MI, US: Wayne State University Press.

Staff Unzipped. (2019, April 15). #DockersChallengers: Litterati Aims to Clean Up the Planet [blog post]. Retrieved from https://www.levistrauss.com/2019/04/15/dockerschallengers-litterati-aims-to-clean-up-the-planet/

Stewart, Melissa. (2021). The Singapore Company Tackling Homelessness by Building Solar Homes. CNA Luxury. Retrieved from https://cnaluxury.channelnewsasia.com/people/billionbricks-singapore-company-tackling-homelessness-13634918

STN Blog. (2017, April 10). Recycled Rockets? Company Pioneers the First Reusable Rocket [blog post]. Retrieved from http://sitn.hms.harvard.edu/flash/2017/recycled-rockets-company-pioneers-first-reusable-rocket/

Swant, Marty. (2020). The World's Most Valuable Brands. Forbes. Retrieved from https://www.forbes.com/the-worlds-most-valuable-brands/#7e27af13119c

Thurrott, Paul. (2020, July 28). Microsoft 365 Generated Over $20 Billion in Revenues Last Year [blog]. Retrieved from https://www.thurrott.com/cloud/microsoft-365/238412/microsoft-365-generated-over-20-billion-in-revenues-last-year#:~:text=The%20growth%20is%20just%20as,revenues%20in%20just%20one%20year

Van Gelder, K. (2021, January 8). Lawn Mower Market Value Worldwide from 2018 to 2027. Retrieved from https://www.statista.com/statistics/994919/lawn-mower-market-value-worldwide/

Various Articles. (n.d.). In Wikipedia. Retrieved 2020 from https://en.wikipedia.org/wiki/Main_Page

Various Listings. (n.d.). In Yahoo! Finance. Retrieved 2020 from https://finance.yahoo.com/

Varner, M. (2015, January 20). Tech Entrepreneur Uses Instagram to Tackle Waste [blog post]. Retrieved from https://www.nationalgeographic.com/culture/food/the-plate/2015/01/20/instagram-social-media-social-good/

Verma, M., Negandhi, D., Khanna, C., Edgaonkar, A., David, A., Kadekodi, G., Costanza, R., Gopal, R., Bonal, B., Yadav, S., and Kumar, S. (2017). Making the Hidden Visible: Economic Valuation of Tiger Reserves in India. Ecosystem Services (vol. 26, part A), pp 236–244. Retrieved from https://doi.org/10.1016/j.ecoser.2017.05.006

Vullings, R. and Heleven, M. (2015). Not Invented Here: Cross-Industry Innovation. Pennsauken Township, NJ, USA: BookBaby.

Webdale, J. (2009, May 11). BBC Revives Celebdaq with Facebook, Twitter [blog post]. Retrieved from https://www.telegraph.co.uk/technology/news/5308707/BBC-revives-Celebdaq-with-Facebook-Twitter.html

Westcott, M., Sato, S., Mrazek, D., Wallace, R., Vanka, S., Bilson, C., and Hardin, D. (2013, Winter). The DMI Design Value Scorecard: A New Design Measurement and Management Model. Design Management Review.

Index

Figure 14.1: Looking for something special?

https://doi.org/10.1515/9783110703009-014

Figure 14.2: See the fusion? Now go make another . . .

www.ingramcontent.com/pod-product-compliance
Lightning Source LLC
Chambersburg PA
CBHW061256220326
41599CB00028B/5668